To my colleague & friend

[redacted]

with best wishes & the

compliments of

[redacted]

THE BACON LECTURESHIP
AT BOSTON UNIVERSITY

FIRST SERIES : 1928

LONDON : HUMPHREY MILFORD
OXFORD UNIVERSITY PRESS

THE CONSTITUTION OF THE UNITED STATES

In some of its Fundamental Aspects

BY

GASPAR G. BACON, LL.B.

MEMBER OF THE MASSACHUSETTS SENATE

CAMBRIDGE

HARVARD UNIVERSITY PRESS

1928

PRINTED AT THE HARVARD UNIVERSITY PRESS
CAMBRIDGE, MASS., U. S. A.

To my Mother

Mrs. Robert Bacon

FOREWORD

ON October 1, 1926, Mrs. Robert Bacon presented to Boston University a substantial sum of money to establish the

GASPAR G. BACON LECTURESHIP
ON THE CONSTITUTION OF THE
UNITED STATES.

The principal is to be kept safely invested as a part of the permanent endowment funds, the income only to be used for an annual course or series of lectures in Boston University. "The purpose of the Lectureship is to stimulate a study of the Constitution of the United States, its antecedents, history and doctrines, together with the results and implications thereof."

The donor stipulated that the lecturer each year should be appointed by the trustees on the nomination of the President of the University. Our first and only choice of lecturer for the initial course was Senator Gaspar G. Bacon. Indeed, it was the hearing of a single lecture of his on the Constitution of the United States that led to the establishment of the Lectureship. He modestly demurred, inasmuch as the Lectureship carries his name. But being acquainted with his knowledge of the subject, we would have chosen him, even though he had had no connection with the establishment of the Lectureship. He is still a young man; a graduate of Harvard College and Harvard Law School; a practising attorney at the Massachusetts Bar; a member of the Massachusetts State Senate; for the past two years chairman of the Senate Committee on Constitutional Law. He has made himself an authority on the subject.

The Lectures which are included in this volume were given in Boston University College of Liberal Arts on the Mondays, Wednesdays and Fridays of two successive weeks, beginning March 21, 1927. They were largely attended and immensely popular. They are a model of clear thinking, cogent and kindling argument, felicitous words and images, lucid and simple expression.

We asked the lecturer to cover in this first course the entire subject. It is our intention to have each year other recognized authorities deal with particular phases of the subject such as the antecedents of the Constitution, or the history and development of the Constitution, or the doctrines of the Constitution, or the implications of the Constitution. This year, the whole subject is covered, and covered in an excellent way.

The wide reading which these lectures deserve will help to make an intelligent citizenry and, by the same token, will make for the stability of constitutional government.

DANIEL L. MARSH
President of Boston University

PREFACE

A VITAL need in America to-day is a better understanding by its citizens of the institutions of their country. It is one of the greatest educational needs of our time. Any system of popular government is based upon the participation of the people in that government. To what extent any particular example of popular government is successful depends largely upon two factors, first, to what extent is the participation by the people general, and second, to what extent is such participation enlightened.

The experiment of popular government in America is still on trial. Our political system has proved successful under simple conditions. It still remains to be seen how it will stand the strain of the vast complications of life which more and more confront us. In 1857, Lord Macaulay, a recognized authority on government, warned us to await the day when our country became thickly settled, and when our industrial problems would be similar to those of England, with intermittent periods of prosperity and periods of acute distress. He declared at that time: "It is quite plain that your government will never be able to restrain a distressed and discontented majority. . . . Your Constitution is all sail and no anchor."

Perhaps our day of dangerous industrialism has not yet arrived. But it cannot be denied that vast economic changes are going on before our very eyes, and that our form of government is being strained and stretched to keep pace with them. There is a constant demand for legislation to cure all evils; there are recurring manifestations of a desire to change our fundamental institutions. Our fear today is not so much from distressed or discontented majorities as it is from ignorant or selfish minorities imposing their will upon indifferent majorities.

Under these circumstances, the need for an educated, enlightened citizenship, which will give to problems of government the same earnest thought and consideration that it gives to its own private affairs, which will study the fundamental principles of the Constitution, is imperative if we wish to perpetuate the form of government that has made the United States the powerful and prosperous nation that she is today. "All free governments," said James Russell Lowell, "whatever their name, are in reality governments by public opinion, and it is on the quality of this public opinion that their prosperity depends." What we are seeking, therefore, is an enlightened public opinion. We are combating the forces of ignorance and the forces of indifference. We are trying to make the average citizen appreciate that his government is something vital to his own welfare; that to understand and support it is to his own interest.

It is the function of the schools and colleges to instill in the youth of the land a proper understanding of the institutions of their country and the right ideals of citizenship, to prepare them as far as possible to take their place in carrying on the great traditions that have been handed down to them. In these days when America is assimilating vast numbers of men and women of foreign races, who are wholly without knowledge of the principles upon which our government was built, it is vastly important that their children be made to understand by careful instruction the aims of the fathers, the great enduring principles which actuated them, and the wisdom which inspired their work. A knowledge of the Constitution of the United States, with its antecedents, history and doctrines, together with the results and implications thereof, is therefore essential.

To give the students of Boston University and others an opportunity to study the Constitution of the United States, this course has been established. Its purpose is to encourage the further study of American politics through a better understanding of the principles of the Constitution. Unfortunately the word "politics" has come to have a limited significance. It is not in this sense that I use it. I apply to it its broad and proper meaning, a word denoting all things pertaining to the affairs of the nation, state, city or town, and the principles, policies, and functions of government. In this sense, it is of vital interest to every American citizen, for the happiness of every American citizen depends largely upon how his government is administered.

In this, the first year of the establishment of this course, I have attempted a general survey of the Constitution, dealing with certain of its more important provisions, aspects, and implications, and leaving to future lecturers, and more distinguished authorities, a more complete study and the task of elaboration and amplification. It is my hope that this brief outline may stimulate a greater interest in our American institutions. I am aware that the material used is not new, and has been dealt with more profoundly in other courses, on government, history, and law in Boston University, and in the works of many authorities, but this simple treatise may nevertheless be useful to the average student. This is but the beginning of a lectureship which has no limits. To have been given the opportunity to deliver the first course thereof is an honor which I shall always proudly cherish.

I make grateful acknowledgment to the many authorities which I have consulted freely, and I am particularly indebted to Professor William B. Munro of Harvard University, and to Mr. Morris Gray, Jr., for reading my manuscript and offering many valuable suggestions.

The fundamental principles and ideals upon which our government was founded are the same today as they were at the beginning of our history, and it is no less true today than it was when solemnly set forth in the Virginia Bill of Rights of 1776, that "a frequent recurrence to the fundamental principles of the Constitution is absolutely necessary to preserve the advantages of liberty and to maintain a free government. The people have a right to require of their lawgivers and magistrates an exact and constant observance of them."

GASPAR G. BACON

BOSTON, MASSACHUSETTS
April 1, 1927

CONTENTS

THE CONSTITUTION OF THE UNITED STATES

I

The Constitutional Convention of 1787

THE five years between 1783 and 1788 have been justly termed "the critical period of American history."

The war with Great Britain had been fought to a successful conclusion by thirteen separate states, acting together only through sheer necessity. The only semblance of central authority was the Continental Congress. This body, composed of representatives of the states voting as states, had assumed all the necessary powers for the carrying on of the war. It had raised an army, borrowed money, issued paper currency, and even contracted an alliance with France. Its authority rested solely upon general necessity and common consent. The Articles of Confederation, establishing its authority and defining its powers, were not actually ratified and put into effect until 1781.

By these Articles of Confederation, the several states formally entered into a "firm league of friendship with each other, for their common defense, the security of their liberties, and their mutual and general welfare." A Congress of delegates was provided for, not less than two or more than seven from any one state, but each state was to have only one vote. The Congress was given power to declare war, make treaties, coin money, establish post-offices, make rules for the administration of the land and sea forces, and borrow money, but no acts for these purposes could be passed without the consent of at least nine of the thirteen states. The states were expressly denied the right to make treaties with any foreign power, or between themselves, to sustain any military or naval force, except the militia, or to engage in war without the consent of the Congress. But each state retained its sovereignty, freedom, and independence, and could exercise every power which was not by these articles expressly delegated to Congress. Congress had no power to raise money by taxation; it could only make requisitions upon the thirteen members of the confederacy in proportion to the assessed value of their respective real estate, and it was provided with no means of enforcing these requisitions. The states not only retained the power to raise money by direct taxation, but also by levying duties on exports and imports, and they, as well as Congress, could issue paper money. There was no executive, beyond the committees which Congress might appoint to work under its own direction, and the only federal courts were such as Congress might designate for the trial of piracies and felonies committed on the high seas, and for determining appeals in cases of capture. The Articles of Confederation could only be amended by the unanimous consent of all thirteen states. "It was a government of the states, not a government of the people. That was its inherent, fundamental, incurable weakness."[1] "I do not conceive," wrote Washington, "that we can exist long as a nation without having lodged somewhere a power which will pervade the whole union in as energetic a manner as the authority of the state governments extends over the several states."

Such was the form of government under which the new nation embarked upon its first voyage — a central government only in name, with no power to pass any measure except by vote of

[1] W. B. Munro, *The Government of the United States* (N.Y., 1925), p. 28.

two-thirds of the states, with no power to deal effectively with interstate or foreign commerce, and with no power to enforce its decrees. It was an independent, but an impotent, league of states. Any state could, and did, disregard the requisitions made upon it, and the only means of enforcement would have involved civil war. Their own debts were of more importance to the states than the national debt. Of the Continental taxes assessed in 1783, only one-fifth had been paid by the middle of 1785. The clause requiring unanimous consent to amend proved an insurmountable obstacle to effective government. In two cases, at least, a single state blocked a proposal by Congress to raise revenue by the imposition of a duty on imports, and this in the face of a financial situation extremely critical. The army was unpaid, and there were whisperings of revolt, and threats to seize the members of Congress and hold them as hostages. At Philadelphia, in June, 1783, Congress was actually driven out of town by a mutinous band of soldiers. It was only through the calm counsel of Washington that a serious uprising was averted.

There were many other instances of the inability of Congress to function. No commercial treaty with England was possible, because each state had its own tariff. Massachusetts and New York had their own navigation acts. The different states made commercial war upon each other. New York imposed impossible duties upon goods transported from Connecticut and New Jersey. Both these states retaliated, and there ensued a series of ruinous measures which paralyzed trade.

Business was at a standstill, financial distress widespread and acute. There was little or no money in circulation. Debts and taxes could not be paid. Most of the states issued large amounts of paper money. The "continental" paper notes which were in circulation had become valueless, hence the origin of the phrase "not worth a continental." The resulting inflation added to the distress. Some states, like Massachusetts, taxed the people heavily to supply their quota to Congress. This caused outbursts and uprisings among the people, who had been driven to frenzy by their sufferings. One particular band of insurgents, under the leadership of an old soldier named Daniel Shays, plundered and pillaged the country-side for many days before it was finally dispersed.

Shays's Rebellion, so-called, was but one manifestation of the chaotic conditions throughout the thirteen states. The new government was powerless, and the American people were rapidly drifting towards anarchy. No wonder that early in 1787 Madison wrote to Randolph: "Our situation is becoming every day more and more critical. No money comes into the Federal Treasury; no respect is paid to the federal authority, and people of reflection unanimously agree that the existing confederacy is tottering to its foundation." And in 1786 Washington wrote to Mason: "I have beheld no day since the commencement of hostilities that I thought our liberties in such imminent danger as at present." That the American Confederacy did not fall to pieces is due largely to the fact that there arose at this crucial time a group of men with sufficient courage and vision to overcome what appeared to be insurmountable obstacles.

In the spring of 1785, there took place in Washington's house at Mount Vernon an important meeting between the representatives of Virginia and Maryland. It came about by invitation of Washington, to adjust certain differences in regard to the navigation of the Potomac River and head waters of the Ohio, but back of it was the conviction that something had to be done to remedy the disastrous commercial relationship between the states. The development of the western country, too, was one of the dreams of Washington. He foresaw the importance of these rich possessions at a time when few men were willing to give them much thought. His fixed determination was to incorporate them into the new nation. To secure the coöperation of the two states most concerned was the first object of the conference, but, led by Washington, it developed into a discussion of other matters of mutual interest — the advantages of a system of uniform duties, the need for a national currency, and suggestions for greater coöperation and united support among the states. Invitations were sent to Pennsylvania and Delaware to join in the discussion. Out of this conference grew the proposal made to all the thirteen states to meet at Annapolis in September of the following year (1786) to discuss the whole commercial situation.

Only five states were represented at this Annapolis meeting, but the way was paved for another convention to be held at Philadelphia the following May. A report, written by Alexander

Hamilton, was adopted, not only recommending the consideration of legislation on the subject of trade, but making the broader suggestion that the convention "devise such further provisions as shall appear necessary to render the constitution of the Federal Government adequate to the exigencies of the Union." Here was the germ of the new national government.

Under Hamilton's influence, it was gradually beginning to be realized that the only remedy for the evils affecting trade must be looked for in broad constitutional changes. The folly of setting each state apart in a water-tight compartment had made itself apparent. The advantages of combination were becoming clearer. Trade necessities, therefore, the demand for improved business conditions, were the dominant factors in bringing about a general consideration of problems of government.

Congress, always jealous of its prerogatives, objected to a convention with any such broad powers. Congress, its members insisted, was the only source from which such proposals could properly emanate. It did, however, finally adopt a resolution approving the convention, but "for the sole and express purpose of revising the

Articles of Confederation," and with the provision that any amendments that might be adopted had to be subsequently agreed to in Congress. Fortunately, both these stipulations were disregarded by the Convention.

The Convention met at Philadelphia on May 25, 1787, in the State House, where, eleven years before, the Declaration of Independence had been signed. Fifty-five men from all the states, except Rhode Island, made up the delegation, and it is not too much to say that, taken altogether, it was a remarkable body. Many of the delegates had risen to positions of great prominence in their own states; most of them had had experience in public affairs. Thirty-nine had been members of the first or second Continental Congress, and eight had already helped to frame the constitutions of their respective states. There were many lawyers, judges, state officers, men of much distinction, as well as doctors, farmers, and merchants. There were also scheming politicians. But on the whole it was a gathering of representative citizens of exceptional ability. They were in no sense supermen. Their average age was only forty-three, and at least four of the leading figures, Randolph, Madison, Gouverneur

Morris, and Hamilton were under forty. Charles Pinckney of South Carolina was only twenty-nine.

Washington, the leading citizen of the United States, was unanimously chosen presiding officer. For calm and wise counsel, and patient forbearance, he was unequalled. The noble words which he uttered to a group of delegates on the eve of the Convention are an inspiration today: "It is too probable," he said, "that no plan that we propose will be adopted. Perhaps another dreadful conflict is to be sustained. If, to please the people, we offer what we ourselves disapprove, how can we afterwards defend our work? Let us raise a standard to which the wise and just can repair. The event is in the hand of God."

Franklin, one of the most brilliant intellects of the eighteenth century, a venerable and beloved man of eighty-one, was a potent influence in calming the troubled waters during that turbulent session.

The ablest delegation, without doubt, was from Virginia. Madison, essentially a scholar in politics, a profound thinker, an indefatigable worker, though of little personality, was more responsible for the Constitution as it was finally adopted than any other single delegate. He has been called "the Father of the Constitution." He early recognized the necessity both for establishing "a due supremacy of the national authority," and for leaving in force local government as well.

Of the other delegates from Virginia, Edmund Randolph, its governor, was the author of the Virginia Plan, and afterwards became the first attorney general of the United States; George Mason, one of the ardent champions of the spirit of democracy, was the author of the Virginia Bill of Rights, and largely responsible for the adoption of the first ten Amendments to the Constitution; and George Wythe, "the great preceptor of the Virginia bar," was an eminent professor of law at William and Mary College.

The Pennsylvania delegation ranked next in ability. There was James Wilson, perhaps the most learned jurist, and a great figure in the Convention, and afterwards a justice of the United States Supreme Court; Gouverneur Morris, brilliant, audacious, though not always wise; and Robert Morris, who, by reason of his financial capacity, had contributed more to the success of the war than any other man except Washington.

Alexander Hamilton of New York, that great

political genius, did not take the conspicuous part in the Convention that his talents warranted. He was handicapped by the obstructive tactics of his two colleagues, and he was absent a large part of the time. The one speech he made, in which he declared: "I have no scruple in declaring that the British Government is the best in the world, and I doubt much whether anything short of it would do in America," did not meet with favor. But once the Constitution was adopted, though there was much in it that he did not approve, he became its leading advocate, and by force of reasoning and eloquent persuasion, secured its ratification by his state in the face of tremendous opposition.

Of the other delegates, William Paterson of New Jersey, the sturdy champion of the smaller states, played an important part, and afterwards sat as a justice of the United States Supreme Court. Roger Sherman of Connecticut, able and sagacious, suggested the compromise which was the basis of the plan adopted. Luther Martin of Maryland, a great advocate, remained to the end a bitter opponent of the Constitution. There were also Ellsworth of Connecticut, later Chief Justice of the Supreme Court of the United

States, Gerry and King of Massachusetts, the eloquent John Rutledge, afterwards a justice of the United States Supreme Court, and the two Pinckneys of South Carolina, all men of ability and influence. It was a gathering of eminent men, most of whom had already made their mark in life. The strength of the Convention lay in the fact that therein were represented many different points of view, different temperaments, and different interests, and the result was a reflection of the composite thought of the new nation. Looking back now, after a period of over one hundred thirty-nine years, we cannot but be impressed with their foresight and wisdom.

The most radical thinkers of the time, particularly Thomas Jefferson, Patrick Henry, and Samuel Adams, theoretical philosophers rather than practical business men, whose somewhat visionary ideas of personal liberty and individual rights would naturally have caused them to oppose any effective central government, were, perhaps fortunately, absent from the Convention.

The Convention once in session, the first rule adopted was the provision for secrecy. It was agreed that nothing should be communicated to the outside world. It was even understood that no disclosure should be made of the proceedings during the lives of the members. And it is remarkable that, with very few exceptions, this rule was rigidly adhered to. Madison, whose valuable notes have since been published, jealously guarded his account of the Convention until his death. In these days of intensive publicity, we can readily appreciate the necessity for keeping the deliberations free from the contaminating influences of current politics. Without such secrecy the Convention could not have accomplished its great work, for the pressure of public opinion would have been too strong. It would have prevented the free expression of opinion by the delegates. Compromises would have been much more difficult with the public listening in. If the bitter disagreements had been known to the world, the Constitution would probably never have been ratified.

The Convention once organized, Governor Randolph of Virginia presented the Virginia Plan, much of which was the work of Madison. While purporting to be a series of amendments to the Articles of Confederation, in conformity with the resolution of Congress, it was in truth a new instrument of government. It provided for a national government with a national legislature of two houses, the lower house to be elected by the people of the states, and the upper house to be chosen by the lower from a panel of names submitted by the various state legislatures, and the members of both houses to be apportioned according to population. Here was a radical departure from the Articles of Confederation, for under the new system the legislature was to represent *the people themselves*, and not the states. This plan meant the destruction of the equality of the states. It would have given Virginia, the largest state, sixteen representatives, whereas Georgia, the smallest state, would have had but one. It was not strange, therefore, that this revolutionary scheme should have been violently opposed. Paterson of New Jersey exclaimed: "Shall I submit the welfare of New Jersey with five votes in a council where Virginia has sixteen? I will never consent to the proposed plan. New Jersey would be swallowed up. I would rather submit to a monarch, to a despot, than to such a fate. . . . Neither my state nor myself will ever submit to tyranny."

To show how far the advocates of a strong central government thought it necessary to go, to remedy the evils of the existing system, the Virginia plan also provided that the national legislature should have power "to legislate in all cases to which the separate states are incompetent, and to negative all laws passed by the several states contravening, in the opinion of the National Legislature, the Articles of Union."

That such a scheme of government could have been seriously urged is the strongest evidence of the chaos which then prevailed. It indicated a violent aversion to the disintegrating Confederation. It went to the other extreme, and without doubt, if adopted, would never have been successful.

The Convention then considered in detail the proposals of the Virginia plan. The essence of the debate which ensued, more on abstract principles than on concrete forms, was the well-defined and fundamental difference of opinion between the so-called Nationalists on the one hand, and the States' Rights party on the other. Madison, Wilson, Gouverneur Morris, Randolph, King, and the Pinckneys were the leaders of the former group, and Paterson, Sherman, and Martin, of the latter. The larger states, Virginia, Pennsylvania, and Massachusetts, were aligned against the smaller ones — New Jersey, Connecticut, Maryland, and Delaware. On the vital question of equal representation in the upper house, the first vote fairly indicated the alignment. Those opposed to complete equality of the states were Virginia, Pennsylvania, Massachusetts, North Carolina, South Carolina, and Georgia; those in favor were Connecticut, New Jersey, Maryland, Delaware, and New York — a vote of six to five in favor of the advocates of a *National* Government rather than a government merely of states. The vote of New York was controlled by Yates and Lansing; Hamilton was the minority member. The main reason which influenced the two Carolinas and Georgia to side with the larger states was that their territory was undetermined in extent, they looked forward to the day when they would be among the larger and more prosperous states, and they were unwilling to put themselves upon an equality for all time with the smaller states.

On June 15, Paterson, on behalf of the smaller states, presented the New Jersey plan. In substance, this was merely a continuation of the old Articles of Confederation, an amplification of the powers of the impotent government. The federal legislature which was proposed, composed of one chamber, was still to represent the states, not the people, each state having one vote. The plan was open to the same objections, and had the same weaknesses, as the existing system. The government remained a mere league of states. Congress was granted additional powers, to be sure, and a limited federal judiciary was provided for, but the vital need for an effective national government — the power over the people themselves in matters concerning the nation — was still lacking.

At this stage in the proceedings, Hamilton made his one speech, an elaborate and well-prepared exposition of government, though radical and unconvincing. His main object was to emphasize the fundamental defects and dangers of the weak existing government. His championship of the government of England, from which his countrymen had just revolted because of its abuses and violations of rights, was not calculated to appeal to the other delegates. His impossible proposals for an executive and a senate elected to serve for life, or during good behavior, were hardly in keeping with the principles of democracy for which there was such prevailing sentiment. Hamilton was young, fearless, with a passion for orderly and stable government, and consumed by an intense conviction that the people as a whole could not be trusted. His strongest instinct was for the orderly achievement of a practical end. He saw no hope except in a strong centralized government. He admired the House of Lords as "a most noble institution." He wished to fashion the Senate after it, as "a permanent barrier against every pernicious innovation." He feared "the amazing violence and turbulence of the democratic spirit."

Hamilton's contribution to the Convention was not considerable, but one cannot but admire his dauntless spirit. It is easy to understand why his plan for an elective monarchy was not even taken seriously.

The difference between the two opposing factions in the Convention was fundamental, and apparently irreconcilable. One side believed that no effective national government could be established, unless it had the power to enforce its decrees against the people. To do this the legislature had to represent the people, not the states. The other side was equally insistent that the equality of the states should be preserved. The smaller states were jealous of their sovereignty. They saw themselves overwhelmed by the larger ones, and at the mercy of the central government. Having just concluded a long and ruinous war to get rid of a foreign tyrant, they saw no good reason to set up a domestic one in its stead. Their sole purpose was to establish a free government which would secure to every person his ancient rights and liberties. On no basis other than equality would they agree to anything. On any other basis, they would leave the convention.

Washington, at this darkest hour, wrote to Hamilton, who had gone home for a few days: "I almost despair of seeing a favorable issue to the proceedings of our convention. . . . The men, who oppose a strong and energetic government, are, in my opinion, narrow-minded politicians, or are under the influence of local views."

There was much bitter feeling; heated words were exchanged, and a rupture seemed inevitable. One delegate suggested that the smaller states find some foreign ally who would take them by the hand and do them justice.

At this point, the venerable Franklin arose, and suggested a recess of three days, in order, as he said, "to let the present ferment pass off, and to afford time for a more full, free, and dispassionate investigation of the subject." And he proposed the appointment of a chaplain, to appeal to "the Creator of the Universe, beseeching Him to preside in our council, enlighten our minds with a portion of heavenly wisdom, influence our hearts with a love of truth and justice, and crown our labors with complete and abundant success."

Franklin's spirit of tolerance had a salutary effect on the Convention, his suggestion was followed, and a recess was taken. Soon after the Convention met again, on July 2, the great compromise of the Convention was formally proposed by the Connecticut delegation, though the scheme had been under consideration for many days. It provided in substance that representation in the lower house should be according to population, but that the Senate should represent the states equally, with the additional proviso that all bills for raising revenue should originate in the lower house. And, to preserve forever this equal representation of the states in the upper legislative body, it was specifically written in the Constitution itself, "that no state, without its consent, shall be deprived of its equal suffrage in the Senate."

This compromise was generally satisfactory to the representatives of the smaller states. They had secured equal representation in at least one branch of the legislature. But it did not satisfy those who, like Madison and Wilson, were urging a strong central government.

Accordingly, a majority of the delegates of Virginia, Pennsylvania, South Carolina, and Georgia — four states — voted against it. Connecticut, New Jersey, Delaware, Maryland, and North Carolina — five states — voted for it. The vote of Massachusetts was a tie, King and Gorham in favor, and Gerry and Strong against. New Hampshire was not yet represented, Rhode Island was never represented, and New York, because of the hostility of Yates and Lansing, the irreconcilables, who had gone home in disgust, was not recorded. Thus the great compromise of the Convention and of the Constitution was adopted on July 16 by the scant margin of five states to four. The vote of one man might have changed disastrously the history of America.

The smaller states had won a victory, but the price they paid for the victory was the creation of a nation, and the granting to that nation of broad national powers. Little did they appreciate at the time how vast these powers were destined to become.

The larger states had also won a victory, for before accepting the compromise it had been agreed that the new federal government, unlike the government then existing, was to exert its powers directly upon the individual citizen, through its own laws, officials, and courts. Congress was given the power to establish federal courts with jurisdiction in all cases in which the individual citizen was answerable to the national law. And the courts were charged with the duty of upholding the new Constitution, and applying its provisions in all cases properly presented for determination.

Although the principal difficulty was thus overcome, other important compromises were necessary for an agreement. The vital question of slavery arose to plague the delegates. Were slaves to be included in ascertaining population? It was finally provided that, in determining the basis for representation in the lower house, they should be considered neither as full human beings, nor as property, but that three-fifths of them only were to be counted. This was an arbitrary arrangement to solve a very practical difficulty. At the same time, to allay the fears of the slave-holding states in giving to Congress the unlimited power to tax, including the power to tax the great Southern staples, — tobacco and cotton, — and the unlimited power to impose duties on imports, it was inserted in the Constitution that taxes on exports were forbidden, that the maximum tax on slaves imported was to be ten dollars per head, and that the importation of slaves could not be prohibited before the year 1808. These compromises removed formidable obstacles to the adoption of any constitution.

It must not be thought, however, that the Constitution was the result only of compromise. There was much in it of vital importance upon which there was agreement from the beginning. The disputes in the Convention were over questions essentially political; on the great economic questions most of the delegates were in accord. For instance, there was general acceptance of the clauses giving to Congress the power to raise revenue by taxation, to borrow money on the credit of the United States, and to regulate foreign and interstate commerce. The clause which declares that "all debts contracted and engagements entered into, before the adoption of this Constitution, shall be as valid against the United States under this Constitution, as under the Confederation," and that which prohibits the emission of bills of credit and the impairment of the obligation of contracts by the states were also agreed to with practically no dissent. These were all provisions necessary for the restoration of public credit, for the establishment of economic independence, and for the development of the new nation. The great majority of the delegates were men of property, lawyers, merchants, manufacturers, creditors, holders of public securities, and landowners. The small farmers, debtors, and advocates of paper money were not represented. There was, therefore, little disagreement on the great economic questions at issue between debtor and creditor, between farmer and merchant. The advocates of the repudiation of debts, of interference with the rights of property and contract, were not even heard.[1]

[1] Robert L. Schuyler, *The Constitution of the United States* (N. Y., 1923), pp. 109 ff.

The Convention had now been in session for over three months. On September 8, the draft of the Committee on Detail was approved, and on September 12, the Committee on Style reported. Gouverneur Morris is largely responsible for the terse and lucid expression of language. On September 17, the Constitution was signed by thirty-nine delegates out of the original fifty-five. Thirteen had gone home, and three — Randolph, Mason, and Gerry — refused to sign.

For us today, after a lapse of all these years, in which the Constitution has been subjected to every conceivable assault, even the test of civil war, and has withstood them all, it is almost impossible to imagine the misgivings with which the framers finally signed that document. Not one of them looked upon it with whole-hearted approval. Many were reluctant to sign. Hamilton affixed his signature with the words: "No man's ideas are more remote from the plan than my own are known to be; but is it possible to deliberate between anarchy and convulsion on one side, and the chance of good to be expected from the plan on the other?" As old Doctor Franklin signed, he stated that there were several parts of the Constitution which he did not then approve, but that he was willing to trust the judgment of others. Finally, it was Washington, who, silent until that day, now, with pen in hand, made the solemn prediction: "Should the states reject this excellent Constitution, the probability is that an opportunity will never again offer to cancel another in peace, — the next will be drawn in blood."

Thus it was that the Constitution was signed in a spirit of doubt, and with little enthusiasm. Very few of the delegates had any real hope for its success; there was serious question whether it would be ratified by the necessary nine states. But they approved it because they were convinced that there was no alternative but anarchy.

The Constitution was forthwith transmitted to the Congress, and by it submitted to the several states for ratification in convention assembled. Thereupon, a new battle began. The smaller states — Delaware, New Jersey, Georgia, and Connecticut — ratified immediately. In Pennsylvania, its opponents succeeded for a time in preventing the calling of a state convention, and, when it was called, in securing a quorum. But the feeling in Philadelphia in favor of the Constitution was so strong that an angry mob finally broke into the houses of some of the hostile members, and literally dragged them to the State House. Under the leadership of Wilson and McKean, the Constitution was ratified. In Massachusetts, ratification was at first opposed by such strong figures as John Hancock and Samuel Adams. The latter, particularly, was unwilling to sacrifice the liberties of his state to the government of the Union. He was, however, won over by assurances that amendments to the Constitution would cure the defects which troubled him. Hancock was brought into line by an appeal to his vanity. If Virginia did not ratify, which he was told would be the case, Washington could not become President, and Hancock had visions of himself in that exalted position. The vote of Massachusetts for ratification was one hundred eighty-seven to one hundred sixty-eight.

The great and violent debates on ratification took place in Virginia and New York. Virginia was the most powerful state in the Union, and although, as it happened, its vote was not recorded until after the necessary nine states had ratified, had it not joined the Union, the Union could not have endured. The forces of the opposition were led by Patrick Henry, Mason, and Richard Henry Lee. Mason, the ablest opponent in any state, was dissatisfied with the Constitution chiefly because it failed to include a bill of rights. Patrick Henry, then the greatest orator in America, fought against ratification to the last ditch. Madison, ably assisted by Randolph, who had been converted, and by John Marshall, required all the force of his powerful intellect and indefatigable industry to secure ratification. This he accomplished by a vote of eighty-nine to seventy-nine.

In New York, an important state geographically and economically, the popular feeling against ratification was strong. If New York failed to ratify, although its vote, too, was not necessary to put the Constitution into effect, the new government could not be successful. Hamilton, being in the minority, thereupon set out upon a campaign to enlighten the people. With the assistance of Madison and Jay, he published a series of papers under the signature of "Publius," designed to demonstrate how the new Constitution offered the only practicable solution for all the difficult problems involved. These papers had a marked influence not only upon the thought of that day, but, collected under the title of "The Federalist," they have survived until the present time, and present a study of the science of government unrivalled in the field of American political literature. Hamilton's service in procuring the ratification of New York is inestimable. Opposed as he was to the Constitution when he signed it, he became its foremost advocate, because there was no choice between it and dissolution. The opposition was led by the powerful machine of Governor Clinton, and included Yates and Lansing. Hamilton's principal supporters were Jay and Livingstone. When told that the vote of the members of the New York convention stood two to one against ratification, he replied: "Tell them the convention shall never rise until the Constitution is adopted." The vote for ratification was by a margin of three.

Thus, at length, was realized the novel conception of a nation living under two separate and distinct systems of laws. The Federal Constitution was devised as the most practicable means of restoring the country to a condition of economic prosperity. The framers were largely men of business and property. They aimed to establish a government which could maintain order within and security without. Let it be remembered, as has been well said, that the Constitution was the expression not only of political faith, but of political fears. Its authors had drawn upon their experiences under their state constitutions and the Articles of Confederation. It was a "bulwark of popular liberty," but it was also a workable document, designed to meet the specific needs of the present, and which could be adapted to those of the future. It was the work, not of theorists, but of sane, practical men. That it has succeeded is a glowing tribute to the wisdom of the fathers. They created "a more perfect union" which has endured, and has prospered beyond their wildest dreams.

II

The Four Corner-Stones of the Constitution

THE Constitution has certain fundamental characteristics. It deals largely with essentials. It outlines our framework of government. It grants certain powers, and withholds others. It preserves the equilibrium between the states and the nation. It recognizes and reaffirms the great principle of local self-government. It safeguards the rights of individuals against governmental interference. It provides for a supreme tribunal to maintain the system which it creates. It establishes the principle of representative government. These fundamental characteristics may be classified under four headings:

1. The constitutional limitations upon the powers of the nation and the states.
2. The division of powers between the three branches of government.
3. The doctrine of judicial review.
4. The principle of representative government.

These are the four corner-stones of the Constitution.

The Constitution is our fundamental, organic law. It is in no sense a legislative code. It was intended to establish our form of government for ages to come. It is not within its province to meet the changing needs of legislation. This is the function of the legislatures. The Constitution was intended to be permanent. Its strength lies in its elasticity, in the fact that it contains only broad provisions which can be adapted and applied by the three branches of the government to varying conditions. It can be amended, but only by the method prescribed in the Constitution itself. This presupposes an overwhelming sentiment of the people themselves in favor of such amendments. The Constitution cannot be tampered with. It was constructed to endure.

The *first* corner-stone of the Constitution is the principle of constitutional limitations upon the powers of government. The sovereign people of the United States, fearing the usurpation or abuse of power, carefully limited their different governmental agencies in the exercise thereof. They did this for their own protection. Government, therefore, is limited in its scope;

it must be confined within bounds. To their government the sovereign people have granted only delegated powers, and they have retained for themselves a great residuum of powers not thus conferred. They have reserved for themselves "an area of liberty" into which government may not enter.

In the nations of Europe, on the other hand, until the recent adoption of the new constitutions by Germany, Poland, and others, the sovereignty was entirely in the hands of the government. Government was all-powerful, and, for the most part, unrestricted. The people had only such rights as they had been specifically given; all others were retained by the sovereign power, whether king or parliament. To what extent the new bills of rights will protect the liberties of the people is still conjectural.

The American doctrine of constitutional limitations was instituted, not only for the purpose of preserving individual rights, but also to keep the two great governmental agencies, the national government and that of the states, within their proper spheres of action. It was therefore necessary to define carefully the limits of each. The people of the United States, acting through the states, ordained and established a constitution. Their general purpose was "to form a more perfect Union." They had experienced the futility of a mere league of states; accordingly, they created a federal nation. It was founded on the assent of the people; but this assent was given by the people, not as individuals composing one entire nation, but as members of the distinct and independent states to which they respectively belonged. It was the assent of the several states, derived from the supreme authority in each state, the people. The people of the several states, therefore, had no intention of impairing or weakening the normal functions of the states. "The preservation of the states," said the Supreme Court, "and the maintenance of their governments, are as much within the design and care of the Constitution as the preservation of the Union and the maintenance of the national government. The Constitution, in all its provisions, looks to an indestructible Union, composed of indestructible states." [1]

The Constitution, then, establishes two systems of government, federal and state. It creates the former, and it recognizes the latter. It de-

[1] Texas *v.* White (1869), 7 Wallace 700.

fines and limits the authority of the one which creates, and it affirms the authority of the other within its proper province. The national government was created for national purposes and with national powers only. These comprise "the irreducible minimum of functions absolutely needed for the national welfare."[1] All other powers are reserved to the states, or to the people. Thus, it is specifically set forth in the Ninth Amendment: "The enumeration in the Constitution, of certain rights, shall not be construed to deny or disparage others retained by the people." And in the Tenth Amendment: "The powers not delegated to the United States by the Constitution, nor prohibited by it to the States, are reserved to the States respectively, or to the people."

Under the Canadian Constitution, the situation is reversed. In Canada, whatever power is not given to the provinces remains with the Dominion Parliament. Furthermore, the central government in Canada has a veto power over provincial legislation.

To preserve inviolate the system of govern-

[1] James Bryce, *The American Commonwealth* (2 vols., N. Y., 1913), I, 324.

ment created by the American Constitution, it is declared in Article six: "This Constitution, and the laws of the United States which shall be made in pursuance thereof; and all treaties made, or which shall be made, under the authority of the United States, shall be *the supreme law of the land;* and the judges in every state shall be bound thereby, anything in the Constitution or laws of any state to the contrary notwithstanding." Thus, the Constitution, and the laws made thereunder, in their proper field of action, stand superior to all state constitutions and all state laws. If any state statute should come in conflict with the Federal Constitution, the former must give way to the superior authority of the latter. But no federal laws are superior unless "made in pursuance of" the Constitution. They cannot transcend its authority. They must be within the express powers granted, or reasonably implied therefrom. As Chief Justice Marshall said of the federal government: "It is acknowledged by all to be one of enumerated powers."

The distribution of powers between the national and the state governments is effected in two ways — positively, by conferring certain powers on the national government, and negatively, by imposing certain limitations upon the states. No powers are conferred upon the states, because they retain all the powers not actually taken from them. There are other powers which are denied to the nation, and to the states, respectively, or to both, essentially for the protection of the people themselves against their own governments. Governmental powers, therefore, may be classified as follows:

Powers vested in the national government alone;
Powers which may be exercised concurrently by both national government and the states;
Powers prohibited to the national government alone;
Powers prohibited to the states alone; and
Powers prohibited to both the nation and the states.

The *first* class of governmental powers — those vested in the national government alone, to the exclusion of the states — forms the basis of the entire jurisdiction of the Congress of the United States. They are contained in the eighteen clauses of Section eight of Article one of the

Constitution. They include all the necessary powers to enable Congress to function. The more important are: the power to levy taxes to pay the debts and provide for the common defense and general welfare of the United States; the power to borrow money; the power to regulate foreign and interstate commerce; the power to declare war, to raise and support armies, to maintain a navy, and to provide for the organization, arming, and calling forth of the militia; the power to coin money and regulate the value thereof; the power to establish post-offices; the power to constitute tribunals inferior to the Supreme Court; and certain powers relating to naturalization, bankruptcy, patents, copyrights, and to the government of the national capital. Lastly, the Congress is given the power "to make all laws which shall be necessary and proper for carrying into execution the foregoing powers, and all other powers vested by this Constitution in the Government of the United States, or in any department or officer thereof."

This last is the great general power which has enabled Congress to exercise effectively the powers with which it has been endowed. It has been frequently invoked. Originally, the scope of this power was seriously questioned. The words "necessary and proper" were variously interpreted. By the strict constructionists, such as Jefferson, those who believed in confining government to its narrowest limits, they were given a limited meaning.

Hamilton, on the other hand, a strong believer in effective government, contended that the national government by this general clause was endowed with all powers necessary for its proper functioning. He propounded the theory of implied powers. He said: "There are express and implied powers, and the latter are as effectually delegated as the former. . . . The only question, then, is this: has the *means* to be employed any natural relation to any of the acknowledged, lawful *ends* of the government? The test of constitutionality lies in the end sought. Is the end included in the expressed powers? If it is so included, the means requisite and fairly applicable are constitutional."

The question of the construction of this "necessary and proper" clause arose first in Jefferson's administration in 1803 over the purchase of Louisiana from France. As the Constitution did not expressly authorize the purchase of territory by the national government, the power to do so was doubted. Jefferson, although the great strict constructionist, nevertheless strongly advocated the purchase. At first, he suggested an amendment to the Constitution to permit it, but, being a resourceful politician, and more desirous to attain his object than to insist upon his theory, he acceded to the views of his opponents. He even urged his adherents to suspend their views temporarily for this particular and useful purpose. The constitutional question was not then before the Supreme Court, but later the power to acquire territory was sustained by this tribunal as necessarily implied both from the power to make war and the power to make treaties.[1]

The "necessary and proper" clause was first construed by the Supreme Court in the case of McCulloch *v.* Maryland, decided in 1819. In 1791, the Bank of the United States was created by Congress in support of Hamilton's financial policy for stabilizing the currency and establishing the national credit. No power to charter a bank or a corporation is expressed in the Constitution. In 1818, Maryland passed a law taxing all banks established without authority from the

[1] American Ins. Co. *v.* Canter (1828), 1 Peters 511.

state. The two questions presented were whether Congress had authority to establish such a bank, and if so, whether Maryland could tax it. The Supreme Court held that "the necessary and proper" clause does not impair the right of Congress to exercise its best judgment in the selection of measures to carry into execution the constitutional powers of the government, that it was within the power of Congress to incorporate a bank for the purpose of carrying out its fiscal operations, and that Maryland had no right to burden the proper activities of the nation.

Chief Justice Marshall's reasoning followed the liberal construction theory advanced by Hamilton rather than the limited views of Jefferson. "Let the end be legitimate," said the Court, "let it be within the scope of the Constitution, and all means which are appropriate, which are plainly adapted to that end, and which are not prohibited, but are consistent with the letter and spirit of the Constitution, are constitutional."

This rule has been consistently followed. The doctrine of implied powers has now been firmly established. To this doctrine is due, in part at least, the ability of the national government to keep pace in legislation with the growth and complex development of the nation during the past century.

The *second* class of governmental powers are those that may be exercised concurrently by both national government and the states. In general it may be said that "where a power has been given to the national government, and is not prohibited to the states, it may be exercised by both concurrently unless Congress assumes exclusive jurisdiction, which it may do whenever the power is one that from its nature cannot be shared by two authorities." The power of taxation is the outstanding example of a concurrent power over which Congress cannot assume exclusive jurisdiction. The power to regulate bankruptcies is an instance of a concurrent power which, if exercised by Congress, excludes state legislation on the subject, because such a power cannot be shared by two authorities. The only case in which concurrent power is expressly given to both national and state governments is in the Eighteenth Amendment. There it is provided that "the Congress and the several states shall have concurrent power to enforce this article by appropriate legislation."

The *third* class of governmental powers — those forbidden to the national government alone — are contained in Section nine of Article one of the Constitution, and in the first ten Amendments thereto. Section nine enumerates ten powers which Congress may not exercise, some of which are also forbidden to the states in Section ten. Thus, the writ of habeas corpus shall not be suspended except when the public safety may require it. This writ is the legal process by which one who is held in restraint can bring his case into court to have the legality of such restraint determined. It was suspended in several instances by President Lincoln where former officers of the army or the government had gone over to the Confederacy, and were active in the North against the Union. Such persons were imprisoned and held without trial. Again, no direct tax shall be laid except in proportion to population. This provision has been changed by the Sixteenth Amendment in respect to a tax on incomes. In commercial regulations no preference shall be given to the ports of one state over those of another. No money shall be drawn from the treasury except on appropriations made by law.

The first ten Amendments, known as the "Bill of Rights," were proposed in Congress, and ratified by the states in 1790, as an additional safeguard to individual liberty, and the rights of property. They are all limitations imposed upon the federal government. The inalienable rights guaranteed to freemen in England by the early charters are here reaffirmed. They were not included in the original constitution because it was not deemed necessary to assert what was then generally recognized. "Why," said Hamilton, "declare that things shall not be done which there is no power to do? Why, for instance, should it be said that the liberty of the press shall be not restrained, when no power is given by which restrictions may be imposed?"[1] But, through the insistence of Mason, Jefferson, and others, this declaration of rights was added to the Constitution in the form of amendments. Religious freedom, trial by jury, freedom of speech, protection from unreasonable searches and seizures, security against excessive bail, excessive fines, and cruel and unusual punishment, the right of any person not to be twice put in jeopardy of life or limb for the same offence, or to be

[1] *The Federalist* (Lodge Edition), No. 84.

compelled in any criminal case to be a witness against himself, the right to be tried for a capital or otherwise infamous crime only on the indictment of a grand jury, except in the military or naval service, and the right not to be deprived of life, liberty, or property without due process of law, or to have one's private property taken for public use without just compensation, were thus preserved inviolate in the fundamental law.

The *fourth* class of governmental powers — those forbidden to the states alone — are contained either in Section ten of Article one of the Constitution, or in the Fourteenth Amendment thereto. Many of the powers denied to the states in Section ten are in Section eight granted to the national government. Of these are the power to make treaties, to coin money, to emit bills of credit to be passed as money, to lay any duties on imports, to maintain troops in time of peace without the consent of Congress, to engage in war or to make any agreement with another state or with any foreign power. Most of these powers had been exercised by the states under the Articles of Confederation, and it was therefore deemed necessary not only to confer them upon the nation but, as a double precaution, to deny them to the states.

One important prohibition to the states in Section ten, which cannot be classed with the above, is that denying the right of the states to pass any law impairing the obligations of contracts. A contract, which was valid at the time it was entered into, cannot be rendered void, or be in any wise impaired, by subsequent legislation by the state, or by any subdivision thereof, unless this is deemed necessary for the general welfare. Many cases have arisen in which states have attempted to evade the obligations of contracts made by them with citizens. The Dartmouth College case, in which Daniel Webster was counsel for the college, is perhaps the most celebrated. A charter had been issued to Dartmouth College by George III in 1769. On the faith of that charter, land was conveyed to this institution and gifts were made to it. In 1816, the legislature of New Hampshire passed an act attempting to amend this charter. The trustees of the college objected and brought suit, and the Supreme Court of the United States held that the legislation impaired the obligations of the contract under which the college came into existence, and had continued to exist, and that this act was therefore unconstitutional and void. Under this principle a charter to a private corporation is considered a contract which cannot be revoked or impaired. This does not imply, however, that no private charter can ever be changed. Like all other private property it can be taken or impaired if and when the public interest so requires. The charters of municipal corporations, or other agents of the state for local administration, are, on the other hand, not considered contracts, and are therefore not protected by this clause in the Constitution.

The other important provision of the Constitution affecting the powers of the states is the Fourteenth Amendment. By this amendment all persons born or naturalized in the United States, and subject to the jurisdiction thereof, are citizens of the United States and of the state wherein they reside. No state is permitted to make any law which shall abridge the privileges or immunities of citizens of the United States; nor shall any state deprive any person of life, liberty, or property, without due process of law, or deny to any person within its jurisdiction the equal protection of the laws.

The *fifth* class of powers, those forbidden both to the states and to the national government, are contained in Sections nine and ten of Article one, and in the Thirteenth, Fifteenth, Eighteenth, and Nineteenth Amendments. Neither government can grant a title of nobility, or tax exports, or pass an ex post facto law, or a bill of attainder. An ex post facto law (after the deed or fact) is a law which makes a crime greater than it was when committed, or which inflicts greater punishment than was prescribed at the time when the crime was perpetrated, or which in general deprives the accused of some protection to which he had become entitled.

A bill of attainder in England was an act of Parliament by which a man was tried, convicted, and disposed of without a jury, and without a hearing in court. His blood was attainted or corrupted legally so that he could not inherit property, nor could his children inherit property from him. This method of punishment was often used during the Revolution.

By the Thirteenth Amendment, slavery and involuntary servitude were abolished in the United States. The Fifteenth Amendment provides that the right of citizens of the United

States to vote shall not be denied or abridged by the United States or by any state on account of race, color, or previous condition of servitude. The Nineteenth Amendment extends this right to women. The Eighteenth Amendment prohibits the manufacture, sale, or transportation of intoxicating liquors within the United States for beverage purposes.

Akin to the fundamental principle of constitutional limitations is the theory of the division of powers between the three departments of government: legislative, executive, and judicial. This is the *second* corner-stone of the Constitution. By such separation of powers, each department acts as a check upon the others. Concentration of power was regarded as fatal to liberty. The origin of the principle has been generally attributed to Montesquieu, who expounded it in his "Spirit of Laws," and there is no doubt that this book very profoundly influenced the political thought of America. But "the general idea of differentiating the functions of government," says Munro, "is as old as Aristotle." Montesquieu said: "Constant experience shows us that every man invested with power is apt to abuse it, and to carry his authority as far as it will go. To prevent this abuse, it is necessary from the very nature of things that power should be a check to power." He then proceeded to explain that, unless the legislative power, the executive power, and the judicial power are each one separated from the others, there can be no liberty.

This principle was followed in the Massachusetts Bill of Rights, attached to the Constitution of 1780, as follows: "In the government of this commonwealth, the legislative department shall never exercise the executive and judicial powers, or either of them; the executive shall never exercise the legislative and judicial powers, or either of them; the judicial shall never exercise the legislative and executive powers, or either of them; to the end it may be a government of laws and not of men." These last ten words were pronounced by Webster to be the greatest words contained in any written constitutional document.

This principle was duly adopted in the Federal Constitution, not expressly as it was in many of the state constitutions, but by implication in its separate treatment of the three branches of government. The opening words of Article one are: "All legislative powers herein granted shall be vested in a Congress of the United States." No legislative powers are otherwise granted.

It will be found, however, that the Federal Constitution, like the state constitutions, in prescribing the method of exercising the powers of government departs from the general principle in several respects. Thus, the President can obstruct legislation by his veto power, and can influence it through messages to Congress. The appointing power of the President and his treaty-making power are subject to the advice and consent of the Senate. The judicial branch of the government is to some extent controlled by Congress. Congress, for instance, provides for all the federal courts below the Supreme Court, and fixes the salaries of the judges. A Congress in disagreement with the President may override his veto by a two-thirds vote. In case of failure of election by the electors, the House chooses the President, and the Senate chooses the Vice-President.

Although we have, therefore, no complete separation of powers, each branch of government has its distinct sphere of action, and the whole is safeguarded by our system of checks and balances. The legislature and the executive act as a check upon each other; the judiciary upon both. All civil officers can be removed from office on impeachment for improper conduct by the House, and conviction thereof by the Senate. The Senate acts as a check upon the House. In theory, the Senate, elected for six years, although only one third of the members at a time, represents the sovereign states equally, and the House, elected every two years, represents the people directly. It was contemplated by the framers that these interests might be diverse. The Senate was the more permanent institution, and considered the more conservative. The fixed four-year term of the President removes him from the whims of politics for that period. He remains in power even though the people indicate their disapproval of his policies at the Congressional election held half-way through his term. In the interest of stability, the Executive is thus safeguarded from the dangers of temporary popular feeling and impulsive action. In the parliamentary governments of Europe, on the other hand, the responsible head can be deposed at will.

The wisdom of this system of checks and balances as a practical scheme of government has been seriously questioned by many, including

President Wilson. Undoubtedly, in some respects, this system is cumbersome and slow, and does not make for efficiency in government. It is sometimes a long and difficult process to secure the passage of measures through both houses of Congress. But, by putting a brake on ill-considered action, it is at least an influence for stability. The framers, be it remembered, were jealous of power and distrusted unrestrained democracy. That fear of unrestrained democracy is just as potent today. There is just as much reason to guard against the abuse of government as there was then. Were there no such system of checks and balances to delay action and give time for reflection, we should be subjected to an even greater flood of legislation than is now the case. Even under our present system, unwieldy as it may be, we are inflicted with a great many radical experiments. Is it not better that a "few good laws should fail of passage, by reason of the cumbrous machinery of legislation, than that the country should be overwhelmed by a destructive flood of unwise legislation?" [1] Is it not better "to endure wrongs than to effect disastrous changes in which the proposed remedy may be

[1] James M. Beck, *The Constitution of the United States*, p. 236.

worse than the evil?"[1] "A majority held in restraint by constitutional checks and limitations," said Lincoln, "is the only true sovereign of a free people."

The *third* corner-stone of the Constitution, which will be discussed more fully in the fifth lecture, is the doctrine of judicial review. It is expressly declared in Article six that the "Constitution, and the laws of the United States which shall be made in pursuance thereof . . . shall be the Supreme law of the land; and the judges in every state shall be bound thereby, anything in the Constitution or laws of any state to the contrary notwithstanding." The courts are thereby specifically entrusted with the duty of upholding the Constitution. It is also provided in Article three that "the judicial power shall extend to all cases arising under the Constitution and laws of the United States." "These two provisions," said Webster, "are, in truth, the keystone of the arch. With these, it is a Constitution; without them, it is a Confederacy."

The necessary implication of these two provisions is that the courts have the power to interpret the Constitution, for otherwise, how would

[1] W. H. Taft, *Liberty Under Law*, p. 21.

they be able to decide in any given case whether a law is or is not in conflict therewith? "This," said Chief Justice Marshall, "is the very essence of judicial duty." Rules of limitation would be useless unless enforced, and the only logical agency to entrust with this duty is the judicial power. Thus, the courts have the power of declaring, when a proper case is presented between parties litigant, that a statute, upon which one of such parties relies, but which contravenes some provision of the Constitution, is unconstitutional, and therefore invalid.

The principle was first recognized in America by state courts with respect to state constitutions. It was first actually applied by the Supreme Court of the United States in Marbury *v.* Madison in 1803. "Certainly," said the Chief Justice, "all those who have framed written constitutions contemplate them as forming the fundamental and paramount laws of the nation, and, consequently, the theory of every such government must be, that an act of the legislature, repugnant to the Constitution, is void."

This doctrine of judicial review has since been invoked in innumerable instances in which either the Congress or the state legislatures have attempted to over-ride the Constitution. It has been applied in many cases for the protection of private rights. If the government attempts to exceed its powers, and thus encroaches upon the rights of some individual citizen, he has recourse to the courts, and, in a proper case, they will intervene to protect these rights. This does not mean that the courts are superior to the executive or the legislature. It means that all three branches of government are subordinate to the will of the people as expressed in the Constitution, and to preserve the people's will, thus expressed, is the peculiar function of the courts. The Supreme Court has thus become the guardian of the liberties of the people. It has kept the Constitution supreme. It has interpreted and given life to its provisions.

The *fourth* corner-stone of the Constitution is the principle of representative government. This principle will be enlarged upon in the sixth lecture. The purpose of the framers was to create a representative republic, and not a pure democracy. Their aim was to guard against autocratic power of all kinds. They saw as much danger from the power of uncontrolled majorities as from other forms of tyranny. They established, therefore, a form of government in which the power was to be exercised by chosen public servants acting for the people as a whole, and within certain prescribed limits.

Our forefathers were familiar with the failure in Athens and in Rome of legislation by direct popular vote. This form of government has been tried without success by peoples of unusually high intelligence. Madison undoubtedly had this in mind when he said that democracies have been found incompatible with personal security or the rights of property. He and his associates were therefore as much concerned with avoiding the dangers of direct government as they were with safeguarding the people from the abuses of monarchy.

The Constitution guarantees to the states a republican form of government. This, and no other, is the kind of government for which the framers intended to provide. If the question is raised, therefore, whether or not some particular state has such a government, or which of two conflicting governments is republican, or whether a given political practice is compatible with a republican form of government, it is for the national legislature, not the courts, to decide.

For this is a political, not a judicial, question. In this case, only the people themselves, through their representatives in Congress, have the power to destroy or preserve one of their vital institutions.

These, then, are the four corner-stones of the Constitution. Upon these fundamental principles has been built the great nation that is ours today. Our governmental structure will be secure as long as its foundations remain firm. It will endure as long as the stones of its four corners withstand the assaults made upon them.

III

Our Dual Form of Government

THERE is nothing more distinctive of America than our dual form of government. Under our Constitutional system, as we have seen, there are two sovereigns, and every citizen owes allegiance to both — to his state and to his nation. In regard to matters which may generally be described as local, the state is supreme; in regard to others, which may generally be described as national, the nation is supreme. In 1787, this was a new theory.

Prior to the adoption of the Constitution of the United States, it had not been thought possible to divide sovereignty, or, at least, to have two different sovereignties moving as planets in the same orbit. Up to that time there had been federated governments, or leagues, but the citizens of the different constituent parts or states owed no direct allegiance to the league, but only to the states of which they were members. The Constitution of the United States established a new conception. While the people remained citizens of their respective states in the sphere of government which was reserved to the states, they became also citizens of the central government in the sphere of government specifically delegated to the central power.

It is probably inaccurate to say that there are two sovereignties unless it is explained what is meant by the term. The truth is that the supreme will finds expression through two channels, through the national government, and through the states. The supreme will is the will of the people. Its sovereignty is absolute and undivided. But the people cannot perform the work of government themselves, so they have delegated to the two governments the task of performing it for them. They have, in this sense, but in no other, divided sovereignty. The sovereign power, the people, has divided its delegated authority between the national and the state governments. This conception of sovereignty was expressed by Chief Justice Marshall. "In America," he declared, "the powers of sovereignty are divided between the government of the Union, and those of the States. They are each sovereign, with respect to the objects committed to it, and neither is sovereign with respect to the objects committed to the other." [1]

By this dual system of government there was devised a workable method of establishing a nation without interfering with the right of the states to govern themselves in respect to all local matters. The nation was endowed with all the powers necessary to enable it to function effectively as a nation, but the states retained all the other powers inherent in government. There was created "an indestructible Union composed of indestructible states."

Local self-government is still one of the cornerstones of our political existence. "It is," said President Coolidge, "one of our most cherished possessions. It is the greatest contributing factor to the stability, strength, liberty, and progress of the nation. The greatest solicitude should be exercised to prevent any encroachment upon the rights of the states." This principle is just as fundamental today as it was when the framers, jealously intent upon preserving the local authority of the states, signed the instrument which they believed accomplished this end. The one danger which most of them feared was the en-

[1] McCulloch *v.* Maryland (1819), 4 Wheaton 316.

croachment of any central power upon this authority. The denial of the right of local self-government was, they knew, the principal cause of the Revolution. They had found from experience that a distant and centralized government could be conducted in defiance of the opinions and wishes of the governed. It was deemed vital, therefore, to preserve for themselves the right to control their own local and domestic affairs. As an inherent right, it was theirs solely and exclusively.

It is common knowledge, however, that, since the early days, the relationship between the nation and the states has materially changed. Particularly, during the last twenty years, there has been an increasing tendency on the part of the national government to encroach upon the powers of the states. The states are no longer permitted to regulate and control many matters which were intended by our forefathers to be within their exclusive jurisdiction. They have been shorn of authority, and the long arm of the central government has been correspondingly strengthened.

The cause of this changed relationship is partly economic and partly political. There is no doubt that the conditions under which the division of powers between the nation and the states is today applied are vastly different from the conditions which confronted the framers of the Constitution. In 1787, each state was a separate community, sufficient unto itself. There was little intercourse between states; the sole interest of the people was their local interest. There was fear then that these separate and self-sufficient communities might fall apart, that the Union might resolve into its constituent elements. To-day, the nation is secure, strong and indivisible. All fears of dissolution were forever dispelled by the Civil War. The doctrine of States' Rights, advocated by Calhoun and others before the War — a very different doctrine from that of States' Rights today — will, fortunately, never again be raised. States' Rights no longer means nullification and secession. It now signifies the preservation of that just and wise balance between local self-government and the central authority.

Today, the interests of the people extend all over the United States. The development of facilities for travel and communication has increased enormously the intercourse between states; there are no interstate tariff duties or other barriers, and the people have been knit together by ties of common interest. The economic trend is towards centralization and unification. We now think nationally; there is an active national consciousness. Politically, also, it has been found that state laws were inadequate to regulate and control business which extends throughout all the states, and that national regulation and control were therefore necessary. So the national government has to some extent taken over the performance of functions which formerly belonged to the states. During the past twenty years Congress has enacted legislation to regulate and control the railroads and other corporations doing an interstate business, the sale of foods and drugs, and to prevent entirely the carrying on of certain businesses deemed to be harmful to morals, such as the sale of lottery tickets and traffic in women. Much more has been attempted, but as all federal legislation must be justified as a legitimate exercise of some federal power, whenever constitutional limits have been exceeded, the courts have been called upon to intervene.

President Roosevelt, always chafing under Constitutional restraints, was the leader of a movement to give effective control to the national government over all activities which to his mind needed regulation. If the power to do so was not to be found in the Constitution, he contended that it should be implied "as inherent in the very fact of sovereignty." This was an entirely different theory from Chief Justice Marshall's theory of implied powers. President Roosevelt asserted: "I believe that in every part of our complicated social fabric there must be either national or state control." He stoutly proclaimed against any twilight zone between national and state activities. He believed that everything which needed regulation should be regulated even though it fell outside the domain of state power, but not within the scope of any express power granted to the nation. The Supreme Court, however, effectively disposed of this untenable theory. For ours is a government under the Constitution, it derives its existence and authority altogether from the Constitution, and Congress has no legislative power which is not either granted, or reasonably implied from some express grant. "This government is acknowledged by all to be one of enumerated powers."

The federal power has been extended at the expense of the states in other ways. The treaty-making power of Congress, for instance, is unlimited. Through this power, Congress has regulated matters which it could reach in no other way. Thus, by means of a treaty with Great Britain, Congress has regulated the migration of birds from Canada, although an act of Congress for the same purpose had previously been declared unconstitutional as being outside of its powers.

But a more far-reaching method for the extension of the federal power has been the stretching of the provisions of the Constitution to cover new fields. The two clauses which have been constantly invoked are the interstate commerce clause and the taxing power. Under the power to regulate commerce among the several states, Congress has enacted, and the Courts have upheld, a great mass of social and economic legislation having to do only remotely with commerce. The Sherman Anti-Trust Act, and other anti-trust legislation, ostensibly mere regulations of commerce, were actually intended to control trusts and monopolies. The Pure Food Act was designed to prevent the adulteration of foods; the Anti-lottery Act was to prevent the sale of lottery tickets; the White Slave Act, to prohibit the transportation of women for immoral purposes. The primary object of these measures was obviously regulation or suppression of the business itself; the regulation of commerce was merely incidental. In other words, beginning with the Lottery case decided in 1903,[1] the Supreme Court has upheld the right of Congress, through the medium of professing to regulate commerce between the states, to regulate the manner of production, manufacture, and sale of certain articles within the states. In the Lottery case, four judges dissented, contending that the statute was unconstitutional because it was not a regulation of commerce, but was an exercise of the police power and so infringed a power reserved to the states by the Tenth Amendment. But the prevailing opinion of the Court was that "Congress has power over transportation among the several states; the power is complete in itself; and Congress, as an incident to it, may adopt not only means necessary but convenient to its exercise, and the means may have the quality of police regulations."[2] And in the case

[1] Champion *v.* Ames (1903), 188 U. S. 321.

[2] Hoke *v.* United States (1913), 227 U. S. 308.

sustaining the validity of the Food and Drug Act of 1906 the Court said: "Congress has the right not only to pass laws which shall regulate legitimate commerce among the states, but has full power to keep the channels of such commerce free from the transportation of illicit or harmful articles, to make such as are injurious to the public health outlaws of such commerce and to bar them from the facilities and privileges thereof." [1]

Under this liberal interpretation of the commerce clause, there seemed practically no limit to the power of Congress to regulate or suppress any activity even remotely connected with interstate commerce. But a limit was finally set beyond which Congress could not go. The question was presented as to whether an act prohibiting transportation, in interstate commerce, of goods made at any factory where children of a certain age had been employed, or employed under certain objectionable conditions of labor, could be sustained under the commerce clause.[2] The court divided five to four. The majority held that this was not a regulation of interstate

[1] Hipolite Egg Company *v.* United States (1911), 220 U. S. 45.
[2] Hammer *v.* Dagenhart (1918), 247 U. S. 251.

commerce, but an attempt to regulate manufacture within the several states contrary to the Tenth Amendment. They distinguished the cases that had gone before by saying that "in each of these instances the use of interstate transportation was necessary to the accomplishment of harmful results," while in the present case the goods shipped were harmless in themselves. The principle established was that "the purposes intended by legislation must be attained consistently with constitutional limitations and not by an invasion of the powers of the states." The Court said that the grant of power to Congress over interstate commerce did not give it authority to control the states in the exercise of the police power over local trade and manufacture.

This case marked the turning point in the extension of the interstate commerce clause. That there is a limit to legislation of this character, and that the states still have rights against encroachment of this kind, is now settled.

The national government has also extended the scope of its taxing power. Congress has the power to tax "to pay the debts and provide for the common defense and general welfare of the United States." Under the heading of "general welfare" the purposes for which taxes may be imposed are obviously very extensive. Congress has taken advantage of this broad power, and, under the guise of taxation, has assumed jurisdiction over the production, manufacture, sale and transportation of many articles within the states. Thus, the taxing power was used to destroy the manufacture of oleomargarine artificially colored to look like butter. The Supreme Court upheld the act of Congress, saying: "The judiciary is without authority to avoid an act of Congress exerting the taxing power, even in a case where to the judicial mind it seems that Congress had, in putting such a power in motion, abused its lawful authority by levying a tax which was unwise or oppressive, or the result of the enforcement of which might be to indirectly affect subjects not within the powers delegated to Congress."[1] Acting under this broad interpretation, Congress attempted to impose a tax of ten per cent (10%) of the net profits of any establishment in which children had worked under conditions prohibited in the act previously invalidated by the Supreme Court. Although this act was entitled "A bill to raise revenue," it was not even

[1] McCray *v.* United States (1904), 195 U. S. 27.

pretended that it was enacted for the purpose of raising revenue. "Congress gave it the appearance of a taxing measure in order to give it a coating of constitutionality."[1] The act was obviously designed to regulate child labor and thereby nullify the former decision of the Court. The Supreme Court distinguished the oleomargarine case, and held the act unconstitutional,[2] on the ground that, on its face, it was apparent that it was a penalty rather than a tax, and an unwarranted attempt to interfere with powers reserved to the states under the Tenth Amendment. "To give such magic," said Chief Justice Taft, "to the word 'tax' would be to break down all constitutional limitation of the powers of Congress and completely wipe out the sovereignty of the States."

Under the Eighteenth Amendment, which prohibits the manufacture, sale, and transportation of intoxicating liquors for beverage purposes, Congress has regulated the prescription by doctors of liquor for medicinal purposes. Congress has restricted the maximum amount which any

[1] Justice Holmes in United States *v.* Jin Fuey Moy (1915), 241 U. S. 394.

[2] Bailey *v.* The Drexel Furniture Company (1922), 259 U. S. 20.

physician may prescribe as medicine to one pint per person within any period of ten days, and prohibits such physician from filling this prescription more than once. This act was attacked as an unwarranted interference with the Constitutional right of a physician, under a certificate granted to him by his state, to practise his profession. It was contended that it was outside of the power granted to Congress over liquor for beverage purposes, and was an invasion of the power of each state to control the practice of medicine within its own borders. The Court, however, by a five to four decision,[1] sustained the act on the ground that the not unreasonable regulation of medicinal liquors is within the power given to Congress by the Eighteenth Amendment to enforce "by appropriate legislation" its prohibition of intoxicating liquors for beverage purposes. This decision obviously qualifies a former decision of the same Court which states that "direct control of medical practice in the states is beyond the power of the Federal Government."[2] The effect of the present decision is that Congress has the power, under the guise

[1] Lambert *v.* Yellowley (1926), 272 U. S. 581.

[2] Linder *v.* United States (1924), 268 U. S. 5, 18.

of enforcing the Eighteenth Amendment, to control directly the professional judgment of a physician, and interfere with its free exercise in the treatment of disease. This removes from each state a power which it has heretofore always exercised — that of prescribing the terms and conditions upon which doctors can practise within its own jurisdiction. It is another instance of federal encroachment.

These cases illustrate the trend towards the extension of the powers of the national government, to the exclusion of the states. This trend has been halted by the Supreme Court in the two Child Labor cases, but there is no telling what new field Congress may still try to invade, by means of, and incidental to, some power which it possesses.

There are other instances of federal encroachment. In 1923, acting under pressure from certain organizations, as is usually the case, Congress passed the Sheppard-Towner Maternity Act. This act established a federal commission of three to supervise the distribution among the states of a large sum of money each year for maternity purposes. Only such states as conformed to the standards and regulations prescribed by this Commission were entitled to receive this contribution. Here is an act of the central government attempting to regulate the conditions of maternity in the several states through a bureau in Washington. It is an effort to take from the states a function which is of most intimate concern to the people of the states. It is a direct subversion of the principle of self-government. The fact that the means of accomplishment is through the lure of state financial aid, which is always tempting, makes it none the less objectionable. If the mothers of America are obliged to entrust themselves to the care of a distant bureaucracy, what, we may ask, becomes of local government?

Equally dangerous to the spirit of self-government is the effort to establish a federal Department of Education. The Education Bill, which is still pending, provides for an appropriation of approximately $100,000,000 for education, half of which is to be used to raise the pay of teachers throughout the country. This is an appealing measure, especially to the teachers, who deserve much more than they now receive. But behind it lies the destruction of a principle of the first importance to our system of government. It is the abdication by the states of their duty to provide for the education of the children entrusted to their care, and to pay adequately those who instruct. It means ultimate control of the public schools of the country by the central government at Washington. No program could be more destructive of the principle of local self-government.

The Maternity Bill and the Education Bill received, and are still receiving, the support of many important and worthy civic and political organizations. To what extent the members of these organizations have expressed their individual views, and have thus delegated to their officers the right to speak for the organization, is by no means certain. It is a common occurrence at legislative hearings for agents to purport to represent great bodies of men and women who in fact have not been even consulted. It is safe to say, however, that there are many persons who, having no opportunity to scrutinize the particular project, will consider that any contribution from the federal government for the benefit of women and children should be gratefully accepted. It is only by careful analysis that the harmful results of measures of this kind will be realized. The care of women, and the education of children, will, in the long run, be better safeguarded by relying upon local public opinion than upon rules and regulations imposed by a central bureaucratic government.

There are other projects involving state aid, some in force, and others agitated. All lead to the supervision and regulation of certain state activities by the federal government. Through bureaus in Washington, and governmental agents travelling through the states, the national government is imposing its will in the field of agriculture, internal improvements, education, infant hygiene, industrial rehabilitation, and in other kinds of social welfare movements. The plan is to offer to the states as much by way of federal aid, for these purposes, as the states will themselves appropriate. At first glance this proposition appears to be a profitable one to the states, enabling them to spend fifty per cent (50%) more than they appropriate. But, on analysis, it proves to be a scheme to pay back to the states part of the money which the federal government taxed them to raise, in return for the right to exercise control over local works and local affairs. It is essentially a form of bribery.

"The sources of Federal taxes are so remote from the local taxpayer that he thinks of these Federal contributions as gifts from Heaven. He forgets that he is always the one who pays."[1] By this method, the richer states, which provide most of the taxes, are induced to contribute to the maintenance of the poorer. In 1925, New York paid nearly twenty-five per cent (25%) of all federal taxes, or approximately $690,000,000, and received as federal aid about $4,000,000, or slightly over five per cent (5%) of the total amount disbursed. Pennsylvania paid $269,000,000, and received back $3,800,000. But both Nevada and Utah received back, as federal aid, over one hundred per cent (100%) of the amounts which they respectively contributed to the federal government. The inequality of the system, however, is comparatively unimportant. But any system which makes one state dependent upon other states for its local maintenance, not only destroys the initiative and responsibility of that state, but also tends to destroy the principle upon which our fabric rests. As President Coolidge has said: "Local self-government ought

[1] Albert C. Ritchie, Address at Iroquois Club, Chicago, Jan. 8, 1926.

not to be infringed by assault, or undermined by purchase. . . . These federal subsidies can be curtailed with benefit to both the federal and state governments." For individuals to be governed in their local and private affairs by a bureaucracy at Washington is bad enough, but let us also remember that without an effective local government, retaining its control over all these local and domestic matters, and depending for its existence upon local public sentiment, the springs from which all progress flows would be dried up. Is not this too great a price to pay for any contribution from the federal government no matter how large?

Another proposal, which was enacted by Congress at the last session, was an amendment to the Federal Estate Tax Law, creating a maximum federal tax on property transferred by death, but permitting any state which had a state inheritance tax to deduct from the federal tax up to eighty per cent (80%) of the levy. This meant that any state having a state inheritance tax would, in order to obtain this bonus of eighty per cent (80%) of the Federal tax, be obliged to pass legislation to this effect, as Massachusetts did. It so happened that a wealthy citizen of

Massachusetts had just died, and the tax authorities in Massachusetts were eager to get as much revenue from his estate as possible. But in any state having no state inheritance tax the whole federal tax is taken by the federal government. The obvious intent of this act of Congress was to compel the states to enact legislation in conformity with its provisions. Again, it is wrong in principle as an unwarranted interference with an inherent right of the states. In fact, the whole idea of a federal estate tax, except as an emergency measure in war time, is wrong anyway. The theory of the tax is that it is levied on the right or privilege of transferring property at death, but as the conditions of this transfer can be imposed, and are imposed, only by the state granting the right, the federal government has no interest which justifies levying a tax. State laws, and state laws only, should govern the ownership, transfer, and disposition of property, including the distribution at death. But the federal government has clung to this tax because of the revenue which it produces. It is hoped that before long it will be abandoned, and that this source of revenue will be left entirely to the states, which are legitimately entitled to it.

Quite recently, the investigations by a committee of the United States Senate of the primary expenses of certain candidates for the Senate has raised the general question of the extent of the control of Congress over the election of its members. The Constitution provides: "The times, places and manners of holding elections for Senators and Representatives, shall be prescribed in each state by the Legislature thereof; but the Congress may at any time by law make or alter such regulations, except as to the place of choosing Senators." Under this clause, Congress undoubtedly has the power to regulate "the times and manner of holding elections for Senators," but the Supreme Court has decided, in the Newberry case,[1] that this does not include primary contests. A primary is no more a part of the election of a Senator than would be any other method by which he succeeded in getting his name on the ballot to be voted on at the subsequent election. Congress, therefore, has no power to control the amount of money which may be expended in the primaries by any candidate for

[1] Newberry *v.* United States (1921), 256 U. S. 232.

the Senate. "The exercise [of any such control]," said the court, "would interfere with purely domestic affairs of the state, and infringe upon liberties reserved to the people."

The qualifications set forth in the Constitution for a Senator are three: he must be thirty years of age, have been for nine years a citizen of the United States, and, when elected, an inhabitant of that state from which he has been chosen. Beyond these, only the respective states have the power to prescribe qualifications. This power is theirs exclusively, and, with the exception of the limitations contained in the Fifteenth and Nineteenth Amendments respecting race, color, and sex, cannot be interfered with. It was the intention of the framers to leave to the states the right to control the elections of their Senators and Representatives, except for the supervisory power of Congress to modify local regulations by a federal law in respect only to the "times, places, and manner of holding" such elections.

Each house of Congress, however, is, by the Constitution, "made the judge of the election returns and qualifications of its own members." The Senate, therefore, has the right to determine whether any Senator-elect was in fact elected, and, if so, whether he possesses the requisite Constitutional qualifications as to age, citizenship, and residence. But how far beyond this the Senate may go in passing upon the fitness of a person duly elected, or in overruling the decision of the state which elects him, as to his qualifications, has not yet been determined. The question at issue today is as to the power of the Senate to prevent from taking their seats, because of alleged irregularities in the primaries, two Senators who have been duly certified by the proper authorities in their respective states as having been legally elected. This question is still unanswered. It will be raised when the Senators-elect from Pennsylvania and Illinois present their credentials at the bar of the Senate.

The last and most dangerous method of seeking to enlarge the powers of the federal government, of which the proposed Child Labor Amendment is a recent example, is through amendment to the Constitution. By the Child Labor Amendment it was proposed to turn over to Congress the power to control the labor of all children under eighteen years of age. The two attempts by Congress to regulate this labor, as we have seen, were frustrated by the Supreme

Court as violations of the Constitution. Those who insisted upon this course, therefore, urged a Constitutional amendment. It was passed by the necessary two-thirds vote of Congress, but when it came before the several state legislatures for ratification, it failed. An active campaign of propaganda was waged in its favor. There was much misinformation, some of it imparted innocently. Some people were more willing to be governed by their emotions than by an analysis of the fundamental question involved. It was sponsored by a great many organizations. Like the Education Bill, it received the support of the Socialists and Communists in the country. The Workers,' or Communist, party sent out an appeal to all their members stating among other things, that "State Legislatures must be compelled to ratify immediately the Child Labor Amendment; Capitalism's Congress and state legislatures must be compelled to pass laws providing full government maintenance of all school children of workers and poor farmers." It is easy to understand why this measure appealed to those advocating socialistic doctrines, for government control of the labor, education, and maintenance of youth is a vital part of the Communist program.

When we observe an intensive campaign, as this was, for some measure of social reform, have we not the right to ask whether this activity is due to a sincere belief in the benefits to be obtained therefrom, or whether it is because the measure fits in with a particular program?

The views of the vast majority of the people, however, prevailed. They saw in this proposal an attempt to undermine our system of government. They foresaw the danger of turning over to a bureaucracy at Washington the control of the youth of the land. Admitting that the conditions of child labor are in some states below a proper standard, the remedy for these evils is not in the destruction of the great principle of local self-government. As President Coolidge has said: "It does not at all follow that because abuses exist it is the concern of the federal government to attempt their reform. Society is in much more danger from encumbering the national government beyond its wisdom to comprehend, or its ability to administer, than from leaving the local communities to bear their own burdens and remedy their own evils."

There are obviously practical reasons for preserving the principles of local self-government.

If we overload the national government with matters which normally belong to the states, it will ultimately break down in its machinery. This country is too large, its people too numerous, its interests, conditions, and climate too varied, and its activity too great, for one central government to carry this burden. There is a limit to the capacity of the national government to transact governmental business effectively. There is certainly a limit to the capacity of the national government to understand local conditions sufficiently well to give the different sections of the country what they need. The local government is in immediate contact with local problems, and therefore better able to deal with them wisely and effectively.

The cost of government is another important consideration. The price we pay for the rising tide of bureaucracy is appalling. Five years after the Constitution was adopted, the cost of operating the federal government was approximately nine millions per year. For the year 1926, it was three and a half billions, or approximately three hundred and ninety times as much.

Again, if we deprive the states of powers which are naturally theirs, and theirs alone, we shall ultimately destroy their local self-government, alter their character as independent states, and reduce them to mere subdivisions, or provinces like those of France.

It was the great historian John Fiske, who, about thirty years ago, said: "If the day should ever arrive (which God forbid) when the people of the different parts of our country shall allow their local affairs to be administered by prefects sent from Washington, and when the self-government of the states shall have been so far lost as that of the departments of France, or even so closely limited as that of the counties of England, — on that day the political career of the American people will have been robbed of its most interesting and valuable features, and the usefulness of this nation will be lamentably impaired." He adds: "Too much centralization is our danger to-day, as the weakness of the federal tie was our danger a century ago." If this was true thirty years ago, how much truer is it today!

State legislatures will not continue to function effectively if they are deprived of responsibility. They will become indifferent, inefficient, and impotent. "You cannot take power away from public bodies without having the character of those bodies deteriorate. . . . You can never develop competent and trusted bodies of public servants by expressing distrust of them, by holding them up to the world as being unworthy of confidence." [1]

If the powers of the states are to be preserved, therefore, and their authority to be continued, the states must exercise their powers. "The only way to maintain the powers of government is to govern." The states cannot shirk their responsibilities, or avoid their duties. It is their function, and theirs alone, to ascertain local public sentiment, to crystallize local public opinion, and to administer to the needs of their people as it is impossible for any other governmental agency to do.

In a country such as ours, dedicated to individual liberty, no system can be effective which is not based on sound and genuine public opinion. The people of the United States will not willingly submit to regulations which do not reflect what they need, but which are imposed upon them by a remote governmental body, not in touch with, not in sympathy with, and uninformed as to

[1] Elihu Root, *Addresses on Government and Citizenship* (Cambridge, 1916), p. 270.

local conditions. They will not tolerate interference with their domestic affairs by federal bureaus with their innumerable inspectors and investigators, often irresponsible and ignorant, continually prying into business which ought to be private, and into affairs which ought to be personal.

The agitation in favor of the Child Labor Amendment has raised the general question of the power and desirability of amending the Federal Constitution. The amending process is prescribed in Article five. In substance it is that Congress may, by vote of two-thirds of both houses, propose an amendment to the Constitution, which amendment will be valid only if, and when, it is ratified by the legislatures of three-fourths of the states. There is an additional right given to the legislatures of two-thirds of the states to compel Congress to call a convention for the purpose of proposing amendments, but this right, up to the present time, has never been exercised. The essence of the power to amend is that there must be an overwhelming demand for the amendment proposed. The founders of our government believed that it was inadvisable to change the framework of government unless the unmistakable sentiment of a great proportion of the people was in favor of it. In their conception no less than three-quarters of the states should express their desire for it before any amendment should be adopted. The framers aimed to guard against hasty or inconsiderate action. They feared the impulse of the moment, and therefore provided for a process which they believed would reflect a genuine, wide-spread, and deliberate demand for an amendment before one was put into effect. "It is not wise," said Elihu Root, "that the people of the United States should contract the habit of amending the Constitution. Stability in our government is a matter of vital concern. No change in our Constitution should be permitted to cast a doubt upon its permanency and inviolability, unless there be the weightiest and most commanding reasons. All presumptions are against it. A heavy burden rests upon those who wish to make the change." . . . "Whenever a proposal is made to change the provisions that affect the relations between the states and the national government, there are special reasons for rejecting it, and a double burden rests upon those who propose it."

"The Constitution," said Chief Justice Marshall, "was intended to endure for ages to come, and consequently to be adapted to the various crises in human affairs. To have prescribed the means by which government should in all future times execute its powers would have been to change entirely the character of the instrument and to give it the properties of a legal code."

In the Eighteenth Amendment, however, we departed from this fundamental conception of the Constitution. For the first time in our history we have incorporated in our organic law an act of legislation, and this in the form of a drastic exercise of the police power. We now have as part of the Constitution a far-reaching legislative provision, encroaching upon the reserved powers of the states, and transferring to the federal government jurisdiction over certain matters of local and domestic concern. Whether we could have attained the result in any other way, or in a more effective way, is not for discussion here. It is the belief of most constitutional lawyers, however, that if federal control over intoxicating liquors was deemed to be necessary, it would have been far better public policy, and more in accord with a proper conception of the Constitution, to have adopted an amendment giving Congress the power to legislate on the subject without legislating directly in the amendment itself. Under such a grant of power, Congress could then have legislated from time to time in response to contemporary public opinion, for it is only when a law is based upon sound and genuine public opinion that it can be made effective. This is not an argument for or against prohibition. It serves merely to point out how, in this instance, we have deviated from the essential character of the Constitution. If our American government is to endure, we must maintain the important distinction which exists between the making of a constitution and the enactment of a statute.

Let us, therefore, pause before we sanction any radical change in our fundamental institutions or in our structure of government. Let us reflect before we discard the vital principle of local self-government. Let us remember what our Constitution is, and was intended to be. If there is manifest a genuine necessity for an amendment, let us amend, but only if the proposed amendment represents the intense conviction of an overwhelming majority of the people, after full discussion and careful deliberation. Let us take to heart the sage advice and heed the warning uttered by Washington in his Farewell Address: "Towards the preservation of your government and the permanency of your present happy state, it is requisite, not only that you steadily discountenance irregular oppositions to its acknowledged authority, but also that you resist with care the spirit of innovation upon its principles, however specious the pretexts. One method of assault may be to effect, in the forms of the Constitution, alterations which will impair the energy of the system, and thus to undermine what cannot be directly overthrown."

IV

What the Constitution Means to the Citizen

THE recognition and preservation of the liberties of the individual citizen by specific limitations upon the power of government is one of the essential characteristics of the Constitution. The Anglo-Saxon ideal of personal liberty was thereby permanently adopted by our forefathers, and has been handed down to us as an essential part of our great heritage. This ideal is today the birthright of every American. It is a fundamental part of our charter of government; it can be impaired only if the people themselves, of their own free will, choose to relinquish their inalienable rights. It is the protection of the humblest individual against his own government; it is our bulwark against autocratic power, and against the impulses of an irresponsible majority.

The framers of the Constitution knew well the dangers of unlimited authority. They were familiar with the history of England from the days when the barons wrung from the unwilling hands of King John the great charter of liberties known as Magna Carta. They knew also that these liberties, even though sanctioned by solemn agreement, were not safe unless protected by some effective means of enforcement. The Magna Carta was no sooner signed than there began an unending struggle to maintain the rights which had thereby been recognized, and the long contest for liberty between the Crown and the people was waged continuously for centuries. The English Bill of Rights of 1688 was another landmark in this struggle. This great document was but an enumeration of fundamental principles and instances of their violation. The people had been constantly subject to flagrant usurpations by the Crown.

The colonists in America had these usurpations fresh in their minds. They had left their mother country to escape from persecution and tyranny. They were seeking a larger measure of civil and religious liberty. They had suffered, too, from the decrees of colonial governors, and from the edicts of Parliament. They had learned from bitter experience that an uncontrolled legislative body was not to be trusted. They could no longer endure repeated violations of their essential liberties, and the Declaration of Independence was their final revolt.

In the Declaration of Independence, executed in 1776, our forefathers set forth the principles which should lie at the base of civil society: "that all men are created equal, and that they are endowed by their Creator with certain unalienable rights, that among these are life, liberty, and the pursuit of happiness. That to secure these rights, governments are instituted among men, deriving their just powers from the consent of the governed."

In the various state constitutions, the first of which were adopted in the same year, these principles were more elaborately enumerated, and in none more effectively than in the Bill of Rights of Virginia of 1776, and in the Declaration of Rights of Massachusetts of 1780. The former, framed by George Mason, was the result of the same historic Williamsburg Convention which proposed the drafting of the Declaration of Independence. It is therein solemnly declared: "That all men are by nature equally free and independent; and have certain inherent rights, of which, when they enter into a state of society, they cannot by any compact, deprive or divest their posterity; namely, the enjoyment of life, liberty, with the means of acquiring and possessing property, and pursuing and obtaining happiness and safety."

With these basic principles thus firmly established in state documents before them, and with the same dread of unrestrained power, the framers adopted as part of their federal Constitution, and almost simultaneously with the adoption of the original articles, the first ten Amendments, or Federal Bill of Rights. But for the positive understanding that these safeguards to individual rights and liberties would forthwith be incorporated in it, the Constitution would never have been ratified by the states. Thus we now have as a vital part of our fundamental law these specific guarantees, established solely for the benefit of the individual citizen, against encroachment by the national government. To obtain a proper understanding of them, and to cultivate a greater appreciation of all the rights secured to him by the Constitution, is, therefore, the citizen's first duty.

The term "citizen" is here used, not in its limited sense, merely as one who is eligible to vote, but in its larger aspect, denoting all members of the body politic who have the right to the protection of the government of the United States. There are technically two kinds of citizenship — that of the United States, and that of the states, but there is another class of persons who have not the full rights of citizenship, but who have been granted the benefits of government. All are included in this discussion of the relation of the Constitution to the individual.

The safeguards provided therein for the protection of the citizen may be divided into three classes: those protecting his person, those securing his liberty of action, and those guaranteeing his rights to property. All three are included in the all-embracing clauses of the Fifth and Fourteenth Amendments, stating, respectively, that neither the federal government nor the states shall deprive a person of his life, liberty, or property without due process of law. These words, now familiar in America, having been construed by the Courts in a great variety of applications at the instance of persons who claimed that their freedom had been unlawfully interfered with, came directly from an English statute of the time of Edward III, which in turn was derived directly from Magna Carta. Therein it was solemnly pledged that "No freeman shall be taken, or imprisoned, or be disseized of his freehold, or his liberties, or his free customs, or be outlawed or exiled, or otherwise destroyed, but by the lawful judgment of his peers, or by the law of the land." The words "due process of law" are equivalent to the words "by the law of the land." Both phrases occur in our organic law. The federal Constitution adopted the former wording, but the older phrase, "law of the land," is still found in the older state constitutions, such as those of Virginia and Massachusetts.

Life, liberty, and property, then, cannot be taken or impaired by the government, unless in accordance with due process of law. This means, in effect, not that any law can be passed in derogation of the rights of life, liberty, or property, but that these rights are secure from interference unless the action of the government is "within the limits of those fundamental principles of liberty and justice which lie at the base of all our civil and political institutions." [1]

The government can act only according to "those judicial forms and usages which by general consent have become essentials of a fair

[1] Hurtado *v.* California (1884), 110 U. S. 516, 535.

judicial process."[1] There can be no arbitrary exercise of its powers. But where the public good, or the general welfare, demands that something be done, private rights must give way. Thus, a state may, in the exercise of its power of eminent domain, take or impair private property for a public use, provided fair compensation is given to the owner for the loss or damage sustained thereby. This recognized power inheres in government because such power is necessary to enable it to function, and for the advancement of the public welfare. It must have the right to acquire land for its public buildings, for public ways, and for other public purposes. But the use must be a public one, and the owner is entitled to a fair compensation for his property. Due process of law excludes the possibility of confiscation. An unwarranted exercise of this right is, therefore, a deprivation of property without due process of law. A state, also, may confer this right upon its subdivisions, and upon corporations engaged in public enterprises, such as railroads, street railways, and other public ser-

[1] W. B. Munro, *The Government of the United States* (N. Y., 1925), p. 349.

vice companies, and it may be exercised by them subject to the same restrictions.

The rights of individuals may likewise be invaded by the states in the exercise of that comprehensive power, known as the "police power," which inheres in state sovereignty. It is that general power which justifies a state government in subordinating the rights of the few to the larger benefits to be obtained for the general public. Thus, a state may provide for the protection of the health, safety, good order, morals, and for the general welfare of the community, and probably also may promote the public convenience or the general prosperity, even though the rights of individuals may thereby be adversely affected. Such action is held to be "due process of law." The possession and enjoyment of private rights is subject to such reasonable conditions as may be imposed by the governing authority for the protection of society. When one becomes a member of society he necessarily parts with some rights or privileges which as an individual, not affected by his relations with others, he might retain. "Even liberty itself, the greatest of all rights, is not unrestricted license to act according to one's own will. It is only freedom from restraint under conditions essential to the equal enjoyment of the same right by others." [1]

The police power is far-reaching, and wide discretion will be granted in its exercise. Under this power, innumerable laws have been enacted, and it is being extended by some of the states to a prodigious extent. No one can doubt the necessity for all kinds of health measures to prevent or lighten disease, nor of safety regulations to make less possible the committing of crimes, or to lessen other dangers to the community, or to protect the public from fraud, nor of laws in the interest of public morals, nor of reasonable supervision of business affected with a public interest, nor of all salutary governmental control for the protection of the wage-earner, nor of a variety of other regulations which have a legitimate relation to the protection of the public, and, in some instances, to the general welfare. But we have gone much further, and have sought to justify the invasion of personal liberty on all manner of unwarranted pretexts. Thus we have seen, recently, arbitrary attempts by statute to interfere with the profession of teaching in the schools. A statute of Nebraska, for instance, forbade the

[1] Crowley *v.* Christensen (1890), 137 U. S. 86.

teaching of any subject except in English. The purpose of this legislation, it was claimed, was to foster a homogeneous people with American ideals, and this was a laudable desire. But its effect was to deprive certain free citizens of the protection of the Constitution. This act was therefore held unconstitutional by the Supreme Court, as an unwarranted interference with liberty. "A desirable end," said the court, "cannot be promoted by prohibited means." [1]

Likewise, an act of Oregon, compelling all children between eight and sixteen years of age to attend a public school, was declared to interfere unreasonably with the liberty of parents to direct the education of their own children. The states have no power "to standardize the children by forcing them to accept instruction from public teachers only." "Rights," said the Supreme Court, "guaranteed by the Constitution may not be abridged by legislation which has no reasonable relation to some purpose within the competency of the state." [2]

Laws regulating the hours of labor in certain

[1] Meyer *v.* Nebraska (1923), 262 U. S. 390.

[2] Pierce *v.* Society of the Sisters of the Holy Name of Jesus and Mary (1925), 268 U. S. 510.

employments have been upheld. In the Bakeshop case,[1] decided in 1905, a decision which, at the time, provoked much discussion, the Supreme Court held unconstitutional a New York Statute forbidding employees in bakeries to work over ten hours a day, on the ground that it was an unwarranted interference with the liberty of contract. The majority of the Court felt that there was no fair or reasonable ground to infer that the public health, or the health of the employees, would be materially endangered if the hours of labor in bakeries were not curtailed. Since that decision, however, the Supreme Court, probably to some extent influenced by public opinion, has upheld an Oregon Statute providing for a similar workday in any mill, factory, or manufacturing establishment.[2] In the opinion in the latter case, no mention was made of the Bakeshop decision; it seems to have been ignored, and thus, by inference, overruled. The Court is now disposed to uphold such regulatory statutes unless the exercise of the police power is manifestly unreasonable or arbitrary.

Legislation restricting the hours of labor for

[1] Lochner *v.* New York (1905), 198 U. S. 45.

[2] Bunting *v.* Oregon (1917), 243 U. S. 864.

women in industry has been uniformly upheld. Women are not yet on an economic parity with men. Laws designed for the protection of the health of women may, therefore, be sustained, even when like legislation is unnecessary for men, and could not be sustained. But minimum wage legislation for women goes beyond the question of health. In 1923, Congress passed an act establishing a Wage Board for the District of Columbia and giving to this Board the power to fix minimum rates for women in any occupation within the jurisdiction so as "to supply the necessary cost of living to any such women and to maintain them in good health and to protect their morals." "This," said the majority of the Court, "is simply and exclusively a price-fixing law, confined to adult women, who are legally as capable of contracting for themselves as men." It gives authority to the Board to set up a standard impossible of practical application with any reasonable degree of accuracy. The Court concludes, therefore, that this is an arbitrary exercise of power prohibited by the Constitution.

A variety of laws, such as Workmen's Compensation Acts, for the benefit and protection of the wage-earner, have been sustained. When a

Kansas statute attempted, however, to prevent any employer from requiring, as a condition of employment, that his employees should not join any labor organization during the time of their employment, it was held to be an unreasonable restriction upon the liberty of contract. The three dissenting justices tried to justify it as within the police power of a state to protect the right of workers to join labor unions, but it is difficult to see how such an interference with the right of employer and employee to make a contract of employment, mutually beneficial and entirely satisfactory, and not in any sense either harmful to the employee or to the community, can be sustained.

The regulation of rates of business affected with a public interest is a proper exercise of the police power. Such regulation is clearly for the protection of the public against unfair charges. But the question as to what businesses are in their nature public, rather than predominantly private, is sometimes one of nice distinction. The business of fire insurance, for instance, has been held to be so far clothed with a public interest as to justify regulation.[1] "This case," said the Court

[1] German Alliance Insurance Co. *v.* Lewis (1914), 233 U. S. 389.

in a recent decision, "marks the extreme limit to which this court thus far has gone in sustaining price fixing legislation." Fire insurance contracts have greater public consequence than ordinary contracts; they affect the whole community. The loss from fire is spread over the country; the disaster to an individual is shared by many. A large section of the public has an interest in the insurance fund raised to guarantee against loss. There are peculiar considerations which govern this business which justify the conclusion of the Court.

In a decision handed down in February, 1927, on the other hand, the Supreme Court took the view that a theatre is not so affected with a public interest as to warrant the fixing of prices of admission.[1] Theatres may be regulated, of course, so as to preserve the peace, insure good order, protect the public morals, and the like, but the fixing of the charges by law is no more permissible than would be similar price-fixing of commodities sold by any other private business. "A business," said the Court, "is not affected with a public interest merely because the public are warranted in having a feeling of concern in respect to

[1] Tyson *v.* Banton (1927) 273 U.S. 418.

its maintenance. Nor is the interest meant such as arises from the mere fact that the public derives benefit, accommodation, ease or enjoyment from the existence or operation of the business. . . . A business or property, in order to be affected with a public interest, must be such, or be so employed, as to justify the conclusion that it has been devoted to a public use, and its use thereby, in effect, granted to the public."

There are limits, therefore, to the power to provide by legislation for the common good at the expense of the individual, and when these limits have been exceeded, and individual freedom of action has thus been arbitrarily interfered with, it becomes the plain duty of the courts, in the proper exercise of their authority, to so declare. There are those who would carry the tenets of paternalism very far, but it is well to remember that there is an important element of safety, there is a factor which makes for progress, in holding fast to the great principle of liberty of contract, so long as this right is exercised reasonably, and under proper safeguards to protect the public when the public needs protection. "To sustain the individual freedom of action contemplated by the Constitution, is not to strike down the common good, but to exalt it; for surely the good of society as a whole cannot be better served than by the preservation against arbitrary restraint of the liberties of its constituent members."[1]

The right to liberty and the right to property, guaranteed by the Fifth and Fourteenth Amendments, are in many cases inextricably bound up together. Any distinction between personal and property rights is invidious. The right to liberty means not only freedom from unlawful restraint of the person, but it includes the right to exercise all the rights of a free citizen, to earn a living in any lawful way, and to keep and dispose of all gains lawfully acquired. Thus the right to liberty includes the right to work and the right of contract; and, in the last analysis, the right to property is also the right to work and enjoy its fruits. Both the right to liberty and the right to property embrace the right to acquire property by any lawful means, and the right to use property for any lawful purpose. Every American citizen, therefore, whatever his position in life, should be vitally interested in preserving both his personal and his property rights. There can be no peace

[1] Adkins *v.* Children's Hospital (1923), 261 U. S. 525.

and no satisfaction without personal liberty, and there can be no happiness unless the fruits of man's labor are rendered secure against governmental interference. "Let not him that is houseless," said Lincoln, "pull down the house of another, but let him work diligently and build one for himself; thus by example assuring that his own shall be safe from violence when built."

The Constitution provides other guarantees of the liberty of action. There are the all-important protections against religious intolerance. Many of our ancestors left their mother country to escape religious persecution and to seek liberty in the new world. There is nothing more vital, therefore, in our system of government, than the established principle that every American citizen is entitled to worship as he chooses. The Constitution declares in the First Amendment that no laws shall be made by Congress prohibiting the free exercise of religion, and, in Article six, that no religious test shall ever be required as a qualification to any office of public trust under the United States. It is thus recognized in our fundamental law that a man's religious convictions are solely his own personal concern, and as such should always be respected. This is the true spirit of America.

Freedom of speech and of the press is equally an American doctrine. No man shall be penalized for expressing his beliefs, or for trying to convince others, provided that his exhortations are not treasonable, or contrary to legislation for the legitimate protection of the government. In the early days of the Republic, the attacks upon those in authority were so violent that a Sedition Act was passed, aiming to prevent the publication of matter tending to bring the government into disrepute or contempt. This act, although unpopular, was upheld by the Courts. During the World War, the Espionage Act likewise imposed penalties on those who interfered with the carrying on of the war, or who published matter disloyal to the government or its officials. Such legislation is justified as necessary and proper to sustain and uphold those entrusted with governmental authority. "The Constitution was adopted to preserve our government, not to serve as a protecting screen for those who, while claiming its privileges, seek to destroy it."[1] There is, then, no absolute freedom of speech.

[1] Schenck *v.* United States (1919), 249 U. S. 47.

"That a state in the exercise of its police power may punish those who abuse this freedom by utterances inimical to the public welfare, tending to corrupt public morals, incite to crime, or disturb the public peace, is not open to question."

There are, in addition, a number of constitutional protections to the person of the individual citizen. They relate chiefly to criminal proceedings. All persons are guaranteed the privilege of the writ of habeas corpus except when the public safety requires its suspension. No person may be held in custody on a criminal charge without the right of securing a trial on the legality of such custody. Bills of attainder and ex post facto laws are prohibited. No person shall be held to answer for a capital or otherwise infamous crime unless on an indictment of a grand jury, except in cases arising in the military or naval service. No person shall be subject, for the same offense, to be twice put in jeopardy of life or limb, nor shall he be compelled in any criminal case to be a witness against himself. The people have a right to be secure in their persons, houses, papers and effects against unreasonable searches and seizures. A man's house cannot be entered upon mere suspicion, but only upon legal warrant issued by a court upon probable cause, and supported by oath. In all criminal prosecutions, the accused shall be tried by a jury, shall be informed of the charges, and be confronted with the witnesses against him, and can obtain his own witnesses and his own counsel. Excessive bail, excessive fines, cruel or unusual punishment, and all forms of slavery or involuntary servitude, except as punishment for a crime, are prohibited.

In the interests of the individual there are other limitations imposed on the government by the Constitution. The great principle of equality, set forth in the Declaration of Independence and in state documents, is recognized in various clauses of the Constitution. Every citizen is entitled to the equal protection of the laws. There is no place in the United States for special privilege or for class discrimination. Whatever our differences in opportunities, capacities, aptitudes, or beliefs, every American citizen stands equal before the law. This principle does not prevent reasonable classification; but it forbids all arbitrary discrimination. Every person within the jurisdiction of a state has the protection of reasonably equal laws. The Fourteenth Amendment, adopted in 1868, was designed primarily to assure to the colored race the enjoyment of all the civil rights which, under the law, were enjoyed by white persons, and to give to that race the protection of the government in that enjoyment, whenever it should be denied by the states. But this amendment has been applied to a far wider field, and has served to protect various persons and classes from unreasonable discrimination and arbitrary classification.

Likewise, the states are prohibited from abridging the privileges and immunities of the citizens of the United States, and of the citizens of other states. All citizens can come and go throughout the United States, and, in whatever part they happen to be, are entitled to the privileges and benefits of government and of law. No state is permitted to discriminate against them in favor of its own citizens. If they are in foreign countries, they can demand the protection of the government of the United States.

The rights of property are further safe-guarded in the provisions of the Constitution, in the Fifth Amendment, forbidding the national government to take private property for public use without just compensation, and, in Article one, Section ten, forbidding the states to impair the obligations of contracts. If private property is taken for public use by the national government, the owner has the protection afforded by the Fifth Amendment.

All contracts between individuals, or between individuals and the state, are protected against impairment by the states. A contractual right once acquired cannot be taken away or adversely affected by subsequent legislation, unless, as in the case of all rights, the public necessity, or the public welfare, requires it.

Through his right to vote the citizen participates in his own government. This right is not granted by the Constitution; it is conferred solely by the separate states, and each imposes thereon its own conditions. But the vote is the citizen's greatest political privilege, and on it depends the maintenance of our fundamental institutions.

The right to vote is not held by all citizens. It is granted to those in each state who satisfy the state requirements, subject only to the Fifteenth and Nineteenth Amendments which declare that the right of citizens to vote shall not be denied or abridged by the United States or by any state on account of race, color, sex, or previous condition of servitude. But there is nothing to prevent it from being denied or abridged by the states for other reasons. A state, for instance, would be within its rights under the federal constitution to restrict the right to vote to those who are able to recite the Constitution from memory.

Citizenship does not confer the right of suffrage, nor is citizenship necessary for its enjoyment. Not many years ago the Constitutions of at least nine states granted this right to persons of foreign birth who had declared their intention to become citizens.

Most states now impose certain literacy tests for their electors, but the requirements, even at national elections, are not uniform throughout the United States. It would no doubt improve the quality of the electorate if an adequate literacy test were applied in more states. But whatever the qualifications for suffrage, the need in America today is for a greater appreciation, by those who are eligible to vote, of their duty to take advantage of this privilege. Only in this way can the citizen take part in the government of his country, receive its benefits, and safeguard his inalienable rights.

The limitations imposed on government for the protection of these rights is distinctly an American conception. In other nations, whatever liberty there was had been granted by the sovereign to the people. They enjoyed only such rights as they were specifically given. All other rights were retained by the granting power. In the United States, as we have seen, the source of power is the people, and they reserve to themselves all powers not actually delegated. The source of authority is from below, not from above. The ungranted power which resides in the people constitutes a limitation upon government. In England, the Parliament is sovereign. It may pass any law it chooses in violation of Magna Carta or the Bill of Rights. Not so in America, for we in America keep the sovereignty in our own hands.

The scope and functions of government, therefore, are not all-inclusive; they are limited. There is much that government was not intended to control, and which it should never undertake. It is impossible to cure all evil by statute. The true conception of the ideals and duties of life can be taught only in the home, in the school, and in the church. When we seek by legislation to supplant these influences, we undermine our whole social structure. President Coolidge has stated: "Industry, thrift, character, are not conferred by act or resolve. There is no substitute for individual effort; nothing can take the place of the rewards of service. Laws are insufficient to endow a nation with righteousness." Yet there is manifest today a tendency on the part of an increasing number of people to rely upon legislation as the remedy for all ills. Regulation and standardization are the cures suggested for everything. Government has become the agency through which the conduct of the individual citizen, in its minutest detail, is regulated. Paternalistic measures are agitated in every legislature. Law, in the modern conception, it would appear, is no longer a system to protect life, liberty, and property, but rather a "scheme for social control, intended to secure the moral well-being of the individual, and generally to secure it by forcing upon all the people what some of the people think their well-being requires."[1] Is it not time to pause and consider anew the true functions of government? "The utmost

[1] Albert C. Ritchie, Address at Iroquois Club, Chicago, January 8, 1926.

that government can do," said Elihu Root, "is measurably to protect men, not against the wrong they do themselves, but against wrong done by others, and to promote the long, slow process of educating mind and character to a better knowledge and nobler standards of life and conduct."

Not only is it futile for government to attempt too much, but it is pernicious and distinctly harmful to the individual citizen. There is no doubt that excessive regulation and excessive standardization weaken character, that undue interference with liberty destroys independence and initiative. Undue reliance upon government removes the need of individual effort, paralyzes energy, and stifles enterprise. Allow the doctrines of paternalism to go too far, and the vigorous national characteristics of our race will disappear.

The United States of America was founded in trial and adversity. Our forefathers at Plymouth and at Jamestown established colonies in the wilderness and had to fight to survive. The men from whom we are descended were of sturdy stock and strong fibre. They survived only through their self-reliance and strength of character. It is these qualities in its individual citizens which make a nation great. No free government can be successful unless it permits, consistently with order and justice, the development of individual initiative, and the free play of all the energies of its citizens. Stifle them by inordinate regulation and by multitudinous rules, changing each day according to the impulse of the moment, and the vigor of the people is gone.

We have developed a mania for legislation. We are suffering from a deluge of laws. There are said to be more than two million enactments today on our statute books. "This," says Professor Munro, "is twenty times as many as are actually enforced." And yet each year we keep adding to this number by the thousands. "The enacting, revising, and amending of laws has become a great national industry." [1] "The prevailing obsession seems to be that statutes, like crops, enrich the country in proportion to their volume. The trouble with much of our legislation is that the legislator has mistaken emotion for wisdom, impulse for knowledge, and good intention for sound judgment." [2] Professor Munro

[1] W. B. Munro, *The Government of the United States* (N. Y., 1925), p. 262.

[2] George Sutherland, Address as President of the American Bar Association, September, 1917.

has well said that we have reached the stage where "our laws are too voluminous to be read, too incoherent to be understood, and often too absurd to be enforced. No man who knows the law today, can guess what it will be to-morrow. He can only be sure that to-morrow it will be different from what it is to-day."[1] America is suffering from an epidemic of over-legislation. As a result, we see evidence on every side of disrespect for law. We see deliberate violations of law by our most respected citizens. We read articles by our highest authorities justifying nullification of laws that are in conflict with public conscience and public opinion.

Is it not time therefore, for public opinion to assert itself and attempt to curb this feverish desire to legislate; this tendency to meddle with private affairs? We must go back once more to fundamental principles, and confine government to its true and effective sphere of action. Only in this way, and by a gradual process of education, can we restore proper confidence in government, with respect for and obedience to its laws.

The progress and prosperity of the United

[1] W. B. Munro, *The Government of the United States* (N. Y., 1925), p. 262.

States has not in the past depended upon the regulation of private affairs or of individual behavior. On the contrary, our tremendous development has been brought about not by government, but by individual enterprise and individual initiative protected and encouraged by government. This country has always been considered the land of opportunity. Let us not allow it to become the land of restriction, oppression, and finally stagnation. The liberty of the individual and the common good are not incompatible; liberty and order are not inconsistent. Both must be preserved; both are essential to the progress, to the security, and to the happiness of the people. Whatever else the Constitution means to the citizen, therefore, it imposes on him the paramount duty "to repel every attempt, however insidious or indirect, to destroy liberty in the name of order, or order in the name of liberty, for the alternative of the one is despotism, and of the other the mob." [1]

[1] George Sutherland, Address as President of the American Bar Association, September, 1917.

V

The Balance-Wheel of the Constitution[1]

THROUGH the one hundred and thirty-nine years of the history of our constitutional government, the Supreme Court of the United States has attained such a vital place in our governmental system, and its powers and functions are now so clearly recognized, that perhaps we fail to realize what an absolute innovation it was when adopted by the Convention of 1787. Never before in history had there existed a court with the powers with which this new tribunal was endowed. How it was created, how its functions were determined, and have since developed, is a subject of immense interest and importance in any consideration of the Constitution.

The Constitution, as we have seen, would never have been accepted had it not been definitely understood that there would be incorporated in it forthwith a Bill of Rights, which would, in the

[1] This title is taken from James M. Beck, *The Constitution of the United States*, Chap. 18.

first place, guarantee the reserved powers of the states, and secondly, protect the individual citizen against the exercise of despotic power by the new central government. The first ten Amendments, introduced for this purpose in the First Congress of 1789 and later adopted, are in reality, therefore, an essential part of the original document. But the enumeration of these guaranties obviously implied some effective means of enforcing them. In the mind of Madison, who offered the Bill of Rights in Congress, there was no doubt as to what this means was to be. "Independent tribunals of justice," he said, "will consider themselves in a peculiar manner the guardians of those rights; they will be an impenetrable bulwark against every assumption of power in the legislative or executive; they will be naturally led to resist every encroachment upon rights stipulated for in the Constitution by the declaration of rights."

No divergent views were presented in Congress; there was no argument. It seemed to be assumed that the enforcement of rights was clearly within the province of the judicial power. Prior to that time there had been various expressions of opinion to that effect. Jefferson had written: "In the arguments in favor of a declaration of rights, you omit one which has great weight with me, the legal check which it puts into the hands of the Judiciary." Hamilton in "The Federalist" had declared: "There is no position which depends on clearer principles, than that every act of a delegated authority, contrary to the tenor of the commission under which it is exercised, is void. No legislative act, therefore, contrary to the Constitution, can be valid. To deny this, would be to affirm, that the deputy is greater than his principal; that the servant is above his master; that the representatives of the people are superior to the people themselves; that men acting by virtue of powers, may do, not only what their powers do not authorize, but what they forbid."

As judicial precedents for the exercise of this power, the framers had before them the decisions and opinions of several state courts. In all these cases, the power of the judiciary to declare inoperative an act repugnant to the Constitution was assumed, and, in some instances, was exercised. In no case was it doubted.

In spite of this authority, it has been expressly declared by some legal writers and others, in recent years, that it was not the intention of the framers to confer upon the courts the power of passing upon the constitutionality of statutes. These critics argue that no such power was granted by the Constitution, either expressly or by obvious implication; that at least four suggestions offered in the Convention advocating this power were voted down; that the few cases in which the doctrine had been enunciated by state courts had been strongly disapproved by the people; that it cannot justly be asserted that many of the members of the Convention knew anything about these decisions or that they thought this power existed; and that the subsequent action of the Supreme Court in assuming to exercise the power was an unwarranted usurpation of authority.

This argument is based upon more than one fallacy. The proposition, which was voted on four times, was not the giving to the courts the power to review judicially acts of legislation, but was a proposal to create a council of revision, composed of the President and the Supreme Court, to revise all legislation.[1] These two prop-

[1] Charles Warren, *Congress, The Constitution, and The Supreme Court* (Boston, 1925), p. 53.

ositions are totally different. Judicial review can only be exercised if and when a statute is called into question in a particular case between two parties; but a veto by the judiciary and the President could be exercised over any statute as soon as such statute was passed. It is true that there was some sentiment in the Convention, led by Madison and Wilson, in favor of the judicial veto, but it received no substantial support. The majority of the delegates clearly saw that the function of the courts, in passing upon a statute, related only to its legality or constitutionality in a given case, properly presented and argued, and that the courts were not concerned with the merits of laws in other respects. That the delegates were opposed to giving the Supreme Court the power to sit with the President in a council of revision on *all* laws — this being essentially an exercise of legislative power — indicates that they deemed it advisable to confine the supreme judicial body to its proper judicial functions, one of which was that of judicial review.

It should be noted, also, that most of the leading figures of the Convention took, at one time or another, a definite stand on this question of judicial review. Among those who recognized this doctrine were Hamilton, Madison, Mason, Ellsworth, Martin, Gerry, Wilson, Wythe, Gouverneur Morris, and Paterson.[1] The power of the courts to pass upon the constitutionality of legislation seems to have been assumed by the majority of the leaders. There is no evidence that any proposal to confer this power specifically on the Supreme Court was even discussed in the Convention. Apparently, this was not deemed necessary.

No better statement is found than that of Paterson, sitting as justice of the Supreme Court on the case of Van Horne's Lessee *v.* Dorrance decided in 1795. He said: "What is a Constitution? It is a form of government, delineated by the mighty hand of the people, in which certain first principles of fundamental laws are established. The Constitution is certain and fixed; it contains the permanent will of the people, and is the supreme law of the land; it is paramount to the power of the legislature, and can be revoked or altered only by the authority that made it. The life-giving principle and the death-doing stroke must proceed from the same hand.

[1] See Charles A. Beard, *The Supreme Court and the Constitution* (N. Y., 1926).

What are the legislatures? Creatures of the Constitution; they owe their existence to the Constitution; they derive their powers from the Constitution. It is their commission; and, therefore, all their acts must be conformable to it, or else they will be void. The Constitution is the work or will of the people themselves, in their original, sovereign, and unlimited capacity. Law is the work or will of the legislature in their derivative and subordinate capacity. The one is the work of the Creator, and the other of the creature. The Constitution fixes limits to the exercise of legislative authority and prescribes the orbit within which it must move. In short, the Constitution is the sun of the political system, around which all legislative, executive, and judicial bodies must revolve. Whatever may be the case in other countries, yet in this there can be no doubt, that every act of the legislature repugnant to the Constitution is absolutely void."

The Judiciary Act, providing for inferior federal courts, was passed by Congress in 1789. Although this act did not directly give full power to any federal court to declare an act of Congress unconstitutional, it did provide for appeal from the highest state courts to the Supreme Court of the United States, if the state court, in passing upon the validity of such an act, should hold it invalid. This was a clear recognition of the Supreme Court's power to review state court decisions. Many of the members of the Congress which enacted this legislation had been members of the Convention of 1787. Ellsworth, later Chief Justice of the Supreme Court, was its leading advocate.

This is additional evidence to show that the power of judicial review must have been considered carefully at that time by the leading statesmen; it indicates that they subscribed to this principle, and intended that the power should be exercised. It must not be forgotten that these men were largely men of affairs and men of property, that they were apprehensive of the power of an uncontrolled majority, and that they would naturally aim to restrict such power in an effective way. It is contrary to all reason to suppose that they were willing to entrust their liberties and their interests to an unrestrained legislature. No, they established in the Constitution a system of checks and balances, and they put their faith in an independent supreme tribunal, empowered to protect their constitutional rights from all improper governmental interference.

In this spirit, the framers incorporated in the Constitution the provisions relating to the judiciary. They declared in Article III, Section 1, that "the judicial power of the United States shall be vested in one supreme court, and in such inferior courts as the Congress may from time to time ordain and establish"; and in Section 2, that "the judicial power shall extend to all cases, in law and equity, arising under this Constitution, the laws of the United States, and treaties made under their authority; to all cases affecting the ambassadors, other public ministers and consuls; to all cases of admiralty and maritime jurisdiction; to controversies to which the United States shall be a party; to controversies between two or more states; between a state and citizens of another state; between citizens of different states; between citizens of the same state claiming lands under grants of different states, and between a state, or the citizens thereof, and foreign states, citizens or subjects.

"In all cases affecting ambassadors, other public ministers and consuls, and those in which a state shall be party, the Supreme Court shall have original jurisdiction. In all the other cases before mentioned, the Supreme Court shall have appellate jurisdiction, under such regulations as the Congress shall make." Under this power, Congress passed the Judiciary Act of 1789, above referred to.

Thus, the first section of Article III of the Constitution specifies in what courts the judicial power of the United States shall be vested, and the second section defines the *extent* of the judicial power. Jurisdiction is given to the courts of the Union in two classes of cases. In the *first*, their jurisdiction depends on the character of the case, whoever may be the parties. This class comprehends "all cases in law and equity arising under this Constitution, the laws of the United States, and treaties made, or which shall be made, under their authority." The plain meaning of this clause would seem to be that the jurisdiction of the court extends to all cases growing out of any provision of the Constitution, to all cases in which any section of the Constitution is in dispute, and it places in the hands of the court the determination of the questions at issue. In the *second* class, the jurisdiction depends entirely on the character of the parties. Diverse citizenship is the essential feature. Controversies between citizens of different states are, obviously, of frequent occurrence, but there has also been much litigation between a state and citizens of another state, and even between the states themselves. Charles Warren,[1] the author of an exhaustive and recognized history of the Supreme Court, is my authority for stating that between 1789 and 1923, there were thirty-nine controversies between states, twenty-six involving disputes as to boundaries or territory, two involving recovery of money due from a state on its bonds, and eleven controversies involving direct injuries alleged to have been committed by one state to another. The fact that the representatives of the states in the Congress which passed the Judiciary Act of 1789 were willing to surrender to the Supreme Court one of the essential rights of state sovereignty — the immunity from suit — indicates to what extent they thought it necessary to compromise "in order to form a more perfect union." They did not intend, however,

[1] Charles Warren, *The Supreme Court and Sovereign States* (Princeton, 1924), p. 38.

as was later apparent, to subject the states to suit brought by an individual citizen of another state, although the language of Article III, Section 2, as held by the Supreme Court in Chisholm *v.* Georgia,[1] clearly includes such a case. For, immediately upon the announcement of that decision, which created great dissatisfaction among the Anti-Federalists, the Eleventh Amendment to the Constitution, specifically prohibiting suits against a sovereign state by citizens of another state, was proposed, and duly ratified by the states in 1798.

It is important to note that there is no express grant of judicial power in Article III, and, therefore, no limitation upon such power. It was recognized as *all* the power usually exercised by courts at common law in the states. The legislative powers exercised by Congress are only the legislative powers granted in the instrument itself, but there is no limit expressed in the Constitution to the judicial power. Article III does not say: "All judicial powers herein granted shall be vested in one Supreme Court and the inferior courts"; it says, "*The judicial power of*

[1] Chisholm *v.* Georgia (1793), 2 Dallas 419.

the United States shall be vested." . . . This must mean the judicial power in its entirety, including everything pertaining to it.[1]

The fact that the judicial power itself, that is, the power which comprises the functions exercised by a court *after* it has obtained jurisdiction, is not defined, would seem to answer those who contend that, if it had been intended to give the Supreme Court the power to hold an act of Congress unconstitutional, this power would have been expressed. Why single out this particular attribute of the judicial power when no other attribute is mentioned? *All* judicial power was vested in the Supreme Court, and in such inferior courts as Congress shall provide for. There is no limit to the judicial power which they may exercise; the only limit is as to the kinds of cases over which they may take jurisdiction. Clearly then, if one of the judicial powers with which a court is endowed is the power to decide whether a given statute is in conflict with the higher law, expressed in the Constitution, the federal courts, as well as the state courts, are possessed of this power, and can exercise it.

[1] See Charles Warren, *Congress, The Constitution, and The Supreme Court* (Boston, 1925), p. 56.

All the foregoing was familiar to Chief Justice Marshall when the case of Marbury *v.* Madison was presented to him for decision in 1803. He had been a member of the Virginia Convention that ratified the Constitution. He had made at least one speech in that Convention in which he declared: "If the government of the United States were to make a law not warranted by any of the powers enumerated (in the Constitution), it would be considered by the judges as an infringement of the Constitution which they are to guard. They would not consider such a law as coming under their jurisdiction. They would declare it void." Marshall was familiar with the judicial opinions of all the courts. He knew well the problems which confronted the framers, their aims, and the spirit and doctrines which underlay the Constitution. He was a learned jurist. Who was there better qualified than he to speak for the Supreme Court of the United States, and to apply for the first time in a decision of that court the principle of judicial review?

The case of Marbury *v.* Madison grew out of an application by Marbury to the Supreme Court for a mandamus compelling the Secretary of State, Madison, to deliver to him a commission as justice of the peace in the District of Columbia — an office to which he had been appointed in the closing days of the Adams administration. Jefferson, the new President, had refused to deliver this commission to a political opponent. The actual decision of the Court was that the authority given to the Supreme Court by the Judiciary Act to issue a writ of mandamus in such a case was not warranted by the Constitution, and the application was on that ground denied. Chief Justice Marshall took the occasion to analyze carefully the doctrines by which he came to his conclusions, and this case became forthwith one of the landmarks in American constitutional law. "The powers of the legislature are defined and limited," he said, "and that those limits may not be mistaken or forgotten, the Constitution is written. To what purpose are powers limited, and to what purpose is that limitation committed to writing, if these limits may, at any time, be passed by those intended to be restrained? . . . The Constitution is either a superior paramount law, unchangeable by ordinary means, or it is on a level with ordinary legislative acts, and, like other acts, is alterable when the legislature shall please to alter it. If the former part of the alternative be true, then a legislative act, contrary to the Constitution, is not law; if the latter part be true, then written constitutions are absurd attempts, on the part of the people, to limit a power in its own nature illimitable. . . . It is emphatically the province and duty of the judicial department to say what the law is. Those who apply the rule to particular cases must of necessity expound and interpret that rule. If two laws conflict with each other, the courts must decide on the operation of each. . . . This is of the very essence of judicial duty."

No further reasoning, or further citation of authority, is necessary to establish this doctrine. It has from the first been a vital part of our constitutional system. The Supreme Court stands today as the bulwark against the passions and impulses of the moment. Without the Supreme Court all our cherished rights would be threatened. Without the Supreme Court, the poor and the weak could be trampled under foot. Without its balance-wheel, the Constitution could not survive.

Yet, even at this late date, the right of the Supreme Court to pass on the validity of a statute has been challenged. This function of the Court has been assailed. When some political or other leader, usually of radical tendencies, or some would-be social reformer, is dissatisfied with some particular decision of the Court, his first impulse is to proclaim that the Court has exceeded its powers, and to demand a constitutional amendment depriving it of this power to pass upon the constitutionality of an act of Congress. He sees no good reason why the Constitution should stand in the way of the attainment of his object. He forgets that if some legislative act should attempt to deprive *him* of some essential right, such as free speech, he would no doubt be the first to loudly claim the protection of the Constitution.

It has recently been proposed to provide by constitutional amendment, that, even if a statute has been held unconstitutional by the Court, yet, if it is enacted a second time, it shall become law in spite of the Constitution. This proposal was seriously urged by the late Senator La Follette. This means, of course, that Congress would have the power to overrule the Supreme Court. It would make Congress the supreme judge. It would allow Congress, by a twice-passed statute, to deprive us of the right to life, and liberty, without due process of law, to establish one religion for all, to do away with jury trials and free speech, to concentrate all power in the central government and abolish the states, to close the courts, to seize private property without paying for it, in fact, to violate all the fundamental and inalienable rights which we now as free citizens enjoy. It may be argued that Congress would not be likely to go so far, but a power once given will sooner or later be exercised, and in moments of passion, under the stress of some heated controversy, or under the blinding influence of some political, sectional, or class appeal, anything is possible. At such moments, the helpless minority would receive no consideration. Are we prepared to place in the hands of Congress the unlimited power, by a twice-enacted statute, to regulate our daily lives in every respect, our wages, our private business, the education of our children, our religion, to legislate on any or all subjects of purely domestic and intimate concern? Unless we are so prepared, it is to our own personal interest to preserve and protect the Constitution of the United States, and not to emasculate the judicial power instituted to safeguard it. "It is not necessary," said President Coolidge, "to prove that the Supreme Court never made a mistake; but if this power is taken away from them, it *is* necessary to prove that those who are to exercise it, would be likely to make fewer mistakes."

The advocates of this proposal contend that Congress is in closer touch with the people, is therefore better able to decide what the people want, and can be more safely entrusted than the courts with the proper enforcement of the people's rights. This argument entirely ignores the fact that it is against usurpation by the people themselves that many of the most vital restraints of the Constitution have been imposed, and to delegate to the body most susceptible to popular clamor the safeguarding of those restraints is to take away from the people all protection. "If people adopt restraints against governmental power and their own hasty and intemperate action, obviously the enforcement of those restraints, to be effective, must be confided to some department of the government, free from the immediate influence of the public and the domination of the government. It is only in this manner that Constitutional provisions may be made supreme." [1]

Another proposal, which has lately been seriously urged by another United States senator, is that seven justices out of nine must concur to hold an act of Congress unconstitutional; that unless seven of the nine justices believe the act to be invalid, it shall be considered valid. In other words, a majority of six judges would not be sufficient to declare an act unconstitutional. This obviously means that the opinion of three justices who decide in favor of a statute, is taken as conclusive, rather than the opinion of six, who decide against it — surely a glaring instance of minority rule. It cannot be justly said that the decision of only three out of nine justices is the decision of the court, for this is contrary to fact. It is the decision of a minority of the Court, which is arbitrarily given the effect of judicial decision by command of Congress. It is a gross perversion by Congress of the judicial power. It places in the hands of three men the power of deciding, in opposition to the views of their six colleagues, that, in a given case, some guaranty of liberty or property has not been impaired. It

[1] A. B. Hall, *Popular Government* (N. Y., 1923), p. 170.

permits these three men to countenance and encourage every new assault upon our personal rights. But it still allows a bare majority of the Court to decide that any given statute is within the Constitution. Is there any logical reason to make the decision of five judges sufficient to sustain a law, but to require seven judges to hold it invalid? Should not the rule be the same in both cases?

This proposal is based on a misapprehension. It has been stated that there have been many five to four decisions holding important acts of Congress unconstitutional, which have produced a vast amount of dissatisfaction among the people. There is no truth in this statement. The fact is, according to Mr. Charles Warren,[1] again, that during its entire existence, the Supreme Court has decided only eight cases holding an act of Congress unconstitutional by a five to four vote, and with none of these decisions was there any particular dissatisfaction. One,[2] rendered just after the Civil War, prevented a gross discrimination against former confederates, and would

[1] Charles Warren, *Congress, The Constitution, and The Supreme Court* (Boston, 1925), p. 183.

[2] Ex parte Garland (1867), 4 Wallace 333.

be universally approved today; another[1] was based upon a defect in drafting the law under consideration, which defect has since been remedied; and two others[2] concerned technical matters of no general interest or importance. The income tax case,[3] holding a tax on income from property to be a direct tax, and therefore unconstitutional, because not apportioned according to population, has been rendered obsolete by the Sixteenth Amendment permitting a federal income tax. This decision did not meet with universal approval at the time, and it is now generally believed that a graduated income tax is an equitable measure, but whether or not it was permitted by the original Constitution was an intricate question of judicial interpretation, and the fact that a majority of the Court came to the conclusion that no power to impose such a tax was granted to Congress, is no just cause for criticizing the Court. This form of taxation was not contemplated by the framers. It could, therefore, be put into effect only by constitutional amendment.

1 Employers' Liability Cases (1908), 207 U. S. 463.

2 Knickerbocker Ice Co. *v.* Steward (1920), 253 U. S. 149; Fairbank *v.* United States (1901), 181 U. S. 283.

3 Pollock *v.* Farmers' Loan and Trust Co. (1895), 158 U. S. 283.

The decision holding stock-dividends to be capital and not income,[1] does not affect the tax burden of the average citizen, and is of no general public interest. The theory therein adopted "that a stock-dividend does not distribute property, but simply dilutes the shares as they existed before" has now been accepted with approval.

The seventh case referred to [2] holds that Congress has no power to regulate the primaries in the several states. Those who believe in the rights of the states to control their own local affairs should approve this decision. Each state is competent to regulate its own primaries without outside interference.

The last case, the first Child Labor case,[3] carries out the same principle. It emphasizes the doctrine that it is not the function of the federal government to interfere with matters of domestic and intimate concern to the people of the states — in this instance, with the care, upbringing, and education of children. Those who at first objected to this decision, did so without much consideration of the great principle of local self-

[1] Eisner *v.* Macomber (1920), 252 U. S. 189.

[2] Newberry *v.* United States (1921), 256 U. S. 232.

[3] Hammer *v.* Dagenhart (1918), 247 U. S. 189.

government involved. It is peculiarly the province of the states to remedy the evils of child labor, and any indirect encroachment upon this right and duty is a serious assault upon our system of government. That the decision of the Supreme Court was correct, is now generally admitted. Indeed, it was emphatically approved by vote of the people in an overwhelming majority of the states.

There is another recent case,[1] decided by a five to three opinion, one justice not sitting, which holds minimum wage legislation for women an undue interference with the liberty of contract. Although this decision has been criticized by some legal writers, it should not be forgotten that it is of vital importance to preserve this great principle of liberty. Once it is permitted by legislation to regulate the wages of private employment, there is no limit to the paternalistic and socialistic schemes which may be attempted.

After all the "thunder of political debate has passed" and the voice of the demagogue has been stilled, the people will come to appreciate that the Supreme Court is an institution ordained and established for their own benefit, and any

[1] Adkins *v.* Children's Hospital (1923), 261 U. S. 525.

subversion of its authority is contrary to their own interests. They have only to think of the innumerable instances in which their rights and liberties have been protected by it. If in some particular case they are dissatisfied, surely this is insufficient reason to destroy the instrument created for their security.

The late Senator La Follette was accustomed to say in public speech that the Supreme Court had "usurped the legislative power" in a number of cases. This is a deceptive and inaccurate statement. If, in a given case between two parties, a particular statute or a particular executive act is held to be in conflict with the Constitution, that statute or that act is declared inoperative as to those parties, because it encroaches upon some right given by the Constitution. This is not a usurpation of legislative power or of executive power. It is distinctly a judicial function to decide which law governs in a particular case presented to the Court for determination. This does not make the Court "superior" to Congress, or to the President. They are all three coördinate branches of the government. They each have their special functions, and "the interpretation of the laws is the proper and peculiar province of the courts." The power of the people is superior to all three, and where the will of the legislature or of the executive stands in opposition to that of the people, as declared in the Constitution, the courts will be governed by the latter.

Lincoln has sometimes been referred to as authority for denying the Court's right to pass upon an act of Congress. Nothing could be further from the truth. The famous Dred Scott case, decided in 1857, is generally cited. The actual decision of the cause presented was that a negro, whether slave or not, could not be a citizen of the United States, and could not therefore bring suit in its courts. This decision was rendered nugatory by the Fourteenth Amendment. But the Court went further, and by way of dictum, attempted to settle by judicial decision a great and burning political issue — the majority holding that Congress had no power to exclude slavery from the Territories. The decision was not only wrong, but, what is worse, the Court was not justified in considering the question at all. It was not necessary for the decision of the issue presented. This was admittedly a flagrant attempt to usurp power, and cannot be defended. It was the sole case in our history in which the court exceeded its powers. If there was ever a decision by a court which justified resistance, or which gave just cause for an attack upon the judicial authority, it was this case.

Lincoln, in his great debates with Douglas, was obliged to deal with this decision. He did so thoroughly. Douglas took the attitude that to question the correctness of it was to resist it, and he charged Lincoln with assaulting the Court. Lincoln clearly stated his position as follows: "We believe as much as Judge Douglas (perhaps more) in obedience to, and respect for, the Judicial Department of the Government. We think its decisions on constitutional questions, when fully settled, should control not only the particular cases decided, but the general policy of the country, subject to be disturbed only by amendments of the Constitution as provided in that instrument itself. More than this would be revolution. But we think the Dred Scott decision is erroneous. We know the court that made it has often overruled its own decisions, and we shall do what we can to have it overrule this. We offer no resistance to it."[1]

Lincoln's conception of the courts, his analysis of their powers and the attitude which should be taken in regard to them, did much to allay the loss of confidence in the Supreme Court which was felt at that time due to the Dred Scott decision. The Court was attacked by all the Northern newspapers. Its standing as a sound judicial body, uninfluenced by political considerations, was seriously impaired. But gradually it has regained its lost prestige, and it is very unlikely, with the experience of this one mistake before it, that it will ever again depart from its strict judicial duty. The Dred Scott case has brought vividly to our attention that it is entirely outside of the authority of the Supreme Court to lay down a rule for political action. This principle has since been consistently followed, and no doubt always will be.

The Supreme Court today has the confidence of the thoughtful people of the United States. That it is not infallible, and, like all other human institutions, makes its mistakes, is acknowledged, but can there be any doubt that the constitu-

[1] Speech delivered at Springfield, Illinois, June 26, 1857.

tional rights of the people are safer in its hands than in those of the legislature? It has filled a vital place in the history of our country. It has kept the whole fabric of government together. "It is the cement which has fixed firm the whole Federal structure."[1] It is the guardian of our liberties, and the balance-wheel of the Constitution. Let us ask ourselves, "With all its imagined faults, what is there that can replace it?" What better protection for our institutions could be devised than an independent tribunal of nine judges, appointed by the President and confirmed by the Senate for life, solely on their standing in the legal profession, removed from the whims and storms of party politics, sitting apart, and aiming only to do justice? "Strip this court of its power, and what shall we get in exchange? Discord and confusion, statutes without obedience, courts without authority, an anarchy of principles, and a chaos of decisions, till all law at last shall be extinguished by an appeal to arms."[2]

[1] Charles Warren, *The Supreme Court and Sovereign States* (Princeton, 1924), p. 32.

[2] Idem, *The Supreme Court in United States History* (Boston, 1924), i, 29.

The question which the American people must decide is whether they wish to maintain the guaranties of fundamental rights established in the Constitution for their own benefit. If they do, must they not, of necessity, rely upon the judicial power? Surely, restrictions upon the power of Congress are of little avail if Congress by its own enactment can override them. If these restrictions are to be observed and enforced, is there any other conclusion except that the courts must pass upon the constitutional validity of legislation? There always will be disagreement among judges. In all intricate questions involving the application of the law to different circumstances and different conditions, differences of opinion are unavoidable, but what safer and juster course can be followed than by accepting the prevailing opinion of a majority of a court of law, who have considered carefully all the evidence, and have applied to it full judicial knowledge? Let us remember that it is of no consequence whether or not we agree with any particular decision. What we must determine is whether we wish to submit all questions which affect our individual rights to an impartial judicial tribunal, or to some other organized body. Are we not wiser to place our trust in the independent power of the judiciary, than in the unrestrained will of a representative legislature?

"A sovereign people," said Elihu Root, "which declares that all men have certain inalienable rights, and imposes upon itself the great impersonal rules of conduct deemed necessary for the preservation of those rights, and at the same time declares that it will disregard those rules whenever, in any particular case, it is the wish of a majority of its voters to do so, establishes as complete a contradiction to the fundamental principles of our government as it is possible to conceive. It abandons absolutely the conception of a justice which is above majorities, of a right in the weak which the strong are bound to respect. It denies the vital truth taught by religion, and realized in the hard experience of mankind, and which has inspired every constitution America has produced, and every great declaration for human freedom since Magna Charta — the truth that human nature needs to distrust its own impulses and passions, and to establish for its own control the restraining and guiding influence of declared principles of action."

It is upon these "declared principles of action," formulated solely upon considerations of abstract justice, and unaffected by any concrete interest, that we must rely for the preservation of our rights. "The establishment of this system of fundamental rules, intrusted for their declaration and maintenance to a body of impartial judges, is the great contribution of America to the political science of the world, the great contribution of America to the art of self-government among men." [1]

[1] Elihu Root, *Addresses on Government and Citizenship* (Cambridge, 1916), p. 400.

VI

The Dangers to Representative Government

NICHOLAS MURRAY BUTLER has said recently: "There is under way in the United States at the present time a definite and determined movement to change our representative republic into a socialistic democracy. That attempt, carried on by men of conviction, men of sincerity, men of honest purpose, men of patriotism, as they conceive patriotism, is the most impressive political factor in our public life of today. It strikes at the very root of the government of the United States, and at the principles upon which that government rests. It proclaims a failure that great movement for the establishment of liberty under law, controlled and carried on through the institutions of representative government."

And Elihu Root, speaks of "the great movement which has been going on now in these recent years throughout the country in which our people have been drifting away from their trust in representative government."

That these statements are substantially true cannot be denied. They are the assertions of profound students of American institutions. We are gradually losing sight of the great fundamental principles of representative government upon which this nation was built.

What, then, were the ideals of representative government as conceived by our forefathers? How have we departed from them? Have we advanced or gone backward in our capacity for self-government? These are the questions which strike at the foundations of our political life.

It is clear that the government which was ordained and established by the Constitution of the United States was intended to be, and was, a representative republic, and not a pure democracy. Throughout the debates in the Convention of 1787, and in the Federalist papers, stress is laid upon the difference between these two conceptions of government. Madison wrote: "In a democracy, the people meet and exercise the government in person. In a republic, they assemble and administer it by their representative agents. . . . A republic is a government which derives all its powers directly or indirectly from the great body of the people, and is administered by persons holding their offices during pleasure, for a limited period, or during good behavior. . . . Democracies, wherein the citizens assemble and administer the government in person, have ever been spectacles of turbulence and contention; have been found incompatible with personal security or the rights of property; and have in general been as short in their lives as they have been violent in their deaths."

In the debates in the Convention, Elbridge Gerry of Massachusetts said: "The evils we experience flow from the excesses of democracy." And Hamilton said: "Give all the power to the many, and they will oppress the few. Give all the power to the few, and they will oppress the many. Both, therefore, ought to have the power that each may defend itself against the other. Liberty may be endangered by the abuses of liberty as well as by the abuses of power."

It was the happy medium which our forefathers sought as the ideal system. They knew the history of other forms of government—of Greece, of Rome, of Venice, and of Florence. They had learned from Holland and England the great lessons of civil and religious liberty. They had before them their own experiences in colonial government. They were jealous of the liberties of the people, yet they feared the tyranny of the mob. Thus, the form of government which they adopted was based on a system of checks and balances. The three departments of government were rendered, so far as possible, distinct from each other, yet each could exercise a certain control over the other two. The people could act only through their selected representatives, and the action of these representatives must be within prescribed limits. In the machinery of government which was thus set up, the framers aimed also to make sure that it was the real will of the people which ruled, and not their momentary impulse, their well-considered determination, and not the passing whim or feeling of the hour. They provided for a representative system with two chambers, thus allowing ample time for discussion and reflection, and avoiding, so far as possible, hasty and ill-considered action. In all these provisions, they manifested their fear of the abuse of power, and their distrust of unrestrained democracy.

The instability of conditions and developments in France had a marked influence on American statesmen, and, from the chaos which had followed their own Revolutionary War, they had learned a terrible lesson. They were less concerned about the doctrines of the rights of man than in restoring law and order. A strong central government was vital, a strong government curbed and bridled as far as possible. The emotional phraseology of the Declaration of Independence had given way to stern realities. It is interesting to reflect, as was stated by James M. Beck, that "the Declaration sought in its noble idealism to make the 'world safe for democracy,' but the Constitution attempted the greater task of making democracy safe for the world by inducing a people to impose upon themselves salutary restraints upon majority rule." [1] Perhaps, in the struggles in Europe today, we are witnessing a similar conflict between "noble idealism" and "hard realities."

The framers, therefore, called their new government a *republic*, as distinguished from a *democracy*. While it is true that there are historical examples of different kinds of republics and dif-

[1] James M. Beck, *The Constitution of the United States*, p. 204.

ferent kinds of democracies, the fundamental distinction between these two forms is clear. Our government is often referred to as a "democratic republic," or as a "representative democracy." These terms are paradoxical, and confusing. Atwood says, "There is no such thing as a representative democracy. To use that expression is equivalent to speaking of a 'temperate drunkard.' The very essence of democracy is that the people speak directly. There is no such thing as a 'democratic republic.' To use that expression is equivalent to speaking of 'gluttonous nourishment.' The very essence of a republic is that the people speak through representatives."[1] He concludes, therefore, that the government created by the Constitution was a true republic: "It is," he says, "the golden mean between *autocracy* and *democracy*."

If we understand what kind of government the makers of the Constitution intended to establish, and how they meant to have it function, there is nothing to be gained by over-refinement of language. It is the spirit of the fathers that we are seeking, and as Lord Bryce says: "The spirit of 1787 was conservative, and its constitu-

[1] Harry F. Atwood, *Back to the Republic*, p. 30.

tion was the least democratic of democracies."[1] Certain it is, as Madison so clearly stated, that the framers did not intend to create a democracy in which the sovereign power is exercised by the people directly. They intended to create a republic, "with many and strong constitutional safeguards against the excesses of democracy."[2] As distinguished from other republics, they established what can accurately be described as a "constitutional republic." It was a government which gave the right amount of participation to the people in governmental affairs and insured at the same time the practical working of the governmental machinery and the protection of private rights. This they called a republican form of government, and it is forever secured by Article IV, Section 4, of the Constitution which states: "The United States shall guarantee to every State in the Union a republican form of government."

Yet the republican form of government is in danger today. We hear it stated from time to time that the representative republic fails to reflect public opinion, that our representative

[1] James Bryce, *American Commonwealth* (N. Y., 1913), i, 307.
[2] J. A. Woodburn, *The American Republic*, p. 59.

institutions easily become the prey of the self-seeker, of special interests, of men who would use the public for their own personal advancement or enrichment, and that therefore our system of government must be changed. The change advocated is that we should give the people more direct voice in their own government, that we cannot trust their representatives, that a majority of the people should be able to impose their will, expressed at any given moment, perhaps in emotion, passion, or prejudice, and regardless of the fundamental constitutional guaranties of civil and political liberty. It has been seriously argued that the people themselves should have the power of interpreting the Constitution. In a number of states, constitutional provisions have been adopted taking from the legislatures many of their normal functions, and placing these in the hands of the people themselves by such devices as the initiative, referendum, and recall. The primary system has been enormously extended. The people are required to pass upon complex measures of which they have no knowledge, nor the opportunity to obtain knowledge, and upon candidates too numerous to recognize. Ballots have become so complicated that the average voter turns away in despair. Yet these changes are made, and are advocated, in the name of progress and reform. We are told that if we restore government to a purely democratic form, we shall make it at all times responsive to the public will, and that the abuses which now exist will disappear.

Expedients such as these for bringing about more direct participation by the people in their government are not new. They have all been tried before. Direct legislation by popular vote was familiar in classical times. It led, and has led, to corruption, violence, and disorder, and finally to autocracy and despotism. Direct government on any large scale has been a failure wherever attempted.

The representative principle, on the other hand, is the great contribution of the English-speaking people to the science of government. "It was brought to America by the English colonists. It was the practice of the colonies which formed the Federal Union. It entered into the Constitution as a matter of course, because it was the method by which modern liberty had been steadily growing stronger and broader for six centuries."[1] Through it has come the gradual attainment by the people of political freedom. This great English institution has now been accepted by the self-governing nations of the world.

Any proposal to depart from our system of representative government should be approached, therefore, with the knowledge that it has been advocated before, and was familiar to the framers. It is the fashion to say that the conditions which confronted the men of 1787 have so changed that their views are no longer entitled to weight. But, as concerns changes in the essentials of the Constitution, such a statement is based upon a gross misconception of the character of that document. The framers were not making laws to regulate social and economic conditions. That never was, and is not now, the function of the Constitution. They were supremely wise in confining it, for the most part, to fundamental principles of government, susceptible of adaptation to different needs and conditions. Laws change, as they should, with the march of progress, but fundamental principles do not change. The motives and purposes which actuated the

[1] Elihu Root, *Addresses on Government and Citizenship* (Cambridge, 1916), p. 92.

framers in adopting these principles are of importance today. We should never forget that the men who met in 1787, met with grim determination to save their country from the miseries which threatened it, and to prevent, so far as possible, their recurrence.

One of the dangers which they most feared was the danger from factions. "By a faction," says Madison in "The Federalist," "I understand a number of citizens, whether amounting to a majority or a minority of the whole, who are united and actuated by some common impulse or passion, or of interest, adverse to the rights of other citizens, or to the permanent and aggregate interests of the community." Today we might call such a faction a clique, or a bloc, or any organized portion of the public. Such a faction is generally inspired by some selfish interest contrary to the best interests of the people as a whole. Unfortunately, what Madison feared is a dominant factor in our body politic today. But Madison saw the futility of attempting to remove the causes of faction. As long as there is liberty of thought, which is essential to America, as long as there are clashing interests, there will always be factions. But, realizing this, Madison devoted himself to the task of controlling not the *causes*, but the *effects* of faction. He says, "If a faction consists of *less* than a majority, relief is supplied by the republican principle, which enables the majority to defeat its sinister views by regular vote. . . . When a majority is included in a faction, the form of popular government, on the other hand, enables it to sacrifice to its ruling passion or interest both the public good and the rights of other citizens. *To secure the public good and private rights against the danger of such a faction, and at the same time to preserve the spirit and the form of popular government, is then the great object to which our inquiries are directed.*" Madison concluded that "a pure democracy, citizens who assemble and administer the government in person, can admit of no cure for the mischiefs of faction." He declared, "A republic, by which I mean a government in which the scheme of representation takes place, opens a different prospect, and promises the cure for which we are seeking."

He hopefully placed his faith in a chosen body of citizens, carefully selected by the people, "whose wisdom may best discern the true interest of their country, and whose patriotism and love of justice will be least likely to sacrifice it to temporary or partial considerations."

This, then, is our ideal of representative government — to select as public servants those who have the courage, the ability, and the character, to exercise their own judgment, regardless of factions, and regardless of pressure.

In the final analysis, we must depend for successful government on the due performance by the citizens of their duty at the polls. The people will get the kind of government that they want, or that they take the trouble to insist upon. Ignorance and indifference on the part of the average voter are the real foes of good government. Eternal good citizenship is the price of good government. Good citizenship involves the duty of every man and woman not only to take sufficient interest in the affairs of government to vote, but to know when he or she enters the voting booth who the candidates are, and what the issues are. This sounds simple, but, how many of our citizens fail in this primary and all-important duty! It is a well-known fact that in the United States the percentage of those eligible to vote who actually do vote is below fifty per cent in Presidential elections, and runs as low as ten per cent in less important ones. The percentage in the United States is lower than in all the larger countries of Europe, and is on a par with Mexico and Cuba. Thus, in the greatest self-governing nation in the world, we have a condition of affairs where minorities govern. Surely, if such a large percentage of the people are unwilling for one reason or another to take the trouble to vote for those to whom they entrust their rights and liberties, it is hardly to be expected that they would be more competent or more willing to govern themselves directly had they the opportunity. The truth is that the average American is very little interested in public affairs, unless some matter affects him personally. Then it is probably too late, the damage is done. He protests, he criticizes, he condemns, but to no effect.

The reason for this apparent lack of interest in public affairs has been attributed to various causes. The most obvious is that this is an age of commercialism, that men are engrossed in business or in some profession. America is a nation of vast undeveloped resources, and it is not unnatural that the great majority of men have confined their attention exclusively to industry.

There are other causes. It is stated that the present age is not productive of a political leadership comparable with the past. "Democracy," says Beck, "is an institution which is tempered by wise and noble leadership."[1] Without the leaders, the interest is lacking. There are other pursuits more engaging. As long as the average man can make a living, abstract political issues seem far removed. He is content to let somebody else do the governing.

The American people are, on the whole, prosperous. They certainly have greater advantages than their ancestors, and more opportunities for enjoyment. This is the age of the automobile, the moving-picture, and the radio. Yet, it is also an age of unrest, an age of discontent, of search for excitement, an age in which crime, scandal, and sensation are of great public interest and occupy prominent places in the newspapers. It is an age in which there is little time for reflection. As has been well said, "American civilization devotes so much energy to obtaining the means to make life possible that it has none left to practise the art of living."[2]

[1] James M. Beck, *The Constitution of the United States*, p. 277.
[2] C. E. M. Joad, *Thrasymachus, or The Future of Morals.*

Whatever the cause, there are many persons in America who do not live up to their full duty of citizenship. As a consequence, they are at times represented by men unfitted to represent, and, when some instance of corruption or incompetence is disclosed, they listen to the voice of the self-appointed reformer who advocates some radical change in our institutions. They have neither knowledge themselves, nor sufficient interest even to think for themselves, and yet they are willing to lend a ready ear to misinformation, half-baked truths, and temporary expedients. They know nothing of the history of our government, they know nothing of the experience of the past, and yet they may accept some so-called remedy which has been proved a failure and long since been discarded. There is no greater truth than that contained in the ancient saying: "There is no expedient to which a man will not resort to avoid the real labor of thinking."

The ideal of representative government must depend upon the ability of the American people to produce adequate leadership. The great majority of able men in America devote their talents to other activities than affairs of government. Not so in England. In England, a value not recognized in the United States is set upon public service. An Englishman feels it both his duty and his privilege to devote at least part of his time to the public service. Lord Bryce has said, "The proportion of men of intellect and social eminence who enter public life is much smaller in America than in each of the free countries of Europe."

Surely there is no lack in America of the qualities of leadership; what is lacking is the realization by men of standing that leadership is needed. Nor are there lacking political issues which call for solution. Many of the tremendous problems which confronted Hamilton, Marshall, Webster, and Lincoln have, it is true, been solved. But the work which they began is still unfinished. The fundamental institutions which they established are again threatened. The Supreme Court has been attacked. There are proposals to change the character of the Constitution, to change it from a framework of government, and to give it the properties of a legal code. Washington warned us to "resist with care the spirit of innovation upon its principles, however specious the pretexts." He foresaw that we might be faced with insidious attempts "to undermine what cannot be directly overthrown."

Representative government has been weakened by the initiative, the referendum, and the recall. Legislatures have been restricted by complex state constitutions embodying minute details of legislation which have no place there. The national government has encroached upon the functions of the states. Too much centralization in Washington is a real danger today. Bureaucratic government has grown to abnormal proportions. Socialistic cure-alls are prescribed instead of sound and well-tried remedies. We are losing sight of fundamentals.

In this age of mechanical and scientific progress, the problems of government are becoming increasingly complicated. Man's livelihood is becoming more and more dependent upon the relationship of government to business. There are problems of agriculture, problems of labor, problems of taxation, and many other domestic problems, awaiting wise determination.

In world affairs, the United States has attained a position of influence second to no other nation. Europe is crying out for assistance. In what way can we most effectively help to solve world problems without at the same time sacrificing unduly our own national independence? Whether we wish it or no, the days of isolation are past. We have obligations toward other nations; we have colonial problems in the Pacific; we have duties in the Caribbean Sea; we have relations with Mexico and South America.

Surely, these and others are problems which require for their wise disposition men of capacity, vision, and courage. The assaults upon our form of government call for enlightened statesmanship, and the power to make an unwilling and indifferent people see the truth. The task is to arouse the people to a greater realization of their duties of citizenship, to make the average person appreciate that government is instituted solely for his benefit, depends for its existence upon the consent of the governed, and relies for its successful administration upon the care with which the people exercise their rights.

The remedy proposed by those who are dissatisfied with the present results of government is to take from the public official much of his power and much of his discretion. They would reduce a representative to the position of a mere delegate, solely an agent to carry out the wishes of his constituents. They would instruct him what to do when elected, would pledge him in advance to a definite course of action. They would reduce him from "the status of a real representative chosen by his constituency to give it his experience, his brains, his conscience, and his best service, and make him a mere registering machine for the opinion of the moment, whatever it might happen to be." [1]

This conception of a representative is far different from that contemplated by our forefathers. At the time of the adoption of the Constitution, it was assumed that Congress would be a deliberative body, and that its members would be allowed and expected to use their own judgment. They were chosen to pass upon the various measures proposed, and to decide what was best for the people as a whole. A representative was supposed to be a trustee for the public interest.

Today, unfortunately, there is a tendency to depart from these ideals of public duty. A representative is prone to subordinate his own judgment in an effort to carry out the views or promote the interests of those to whom he owes his election. He sometimes forgets the common good. He may think that it is his duty to do the

[1] Nicholas Murray Butler, *Why should we change our form of Government?*, p. 19.

bidding of his constituents even if he believes that the interests of his state or nation are thereby sacrificed.

Conditions today are no different from those of which Madison wrote in "The Federalist." "Everyone knows," he said, "that a great proportion of the errors committed by the State legislatures proceeds from the disposition of the members to sacrifice the comprehensive and permanent interest of the state to the particular and separate views of the counties or districts in which they reside."

There is the added confusion caused by the direct primary system, which makes it practically impossible for a representative to ascertain and appraise the prevailing sentiment of his district. Under this system, less than twenty-five per cent of the electorate, generally considerably less, can control the nomination of the party's candidates. Thus, we have government by organized minorities, government by factions, classes, or special interests. A representative, who allows himself to be swayed by what he may mistake for genuine public sentiment, may find himself voting not only against his own better judgment, but actually against the judgment and the wishes of a majority of his constituents.

The real duty of a representative has been no better stated than in the classic advice given by Edmund Burke to the electors of Bristol: "It ought to be the happiness and glory of a representative," he said, "to live in the strictest union, the closest correspondence, and the most unreserved communication with his constituents. Their wishes ought to have great weight with him; their opinions high respect; their business unremitted attention. But his unbiased opinion, his mature judgment, his enlightened conscience, he ought not to sacrifice to you, to any man, or to any set of men living. Your representative owes you not his industry only, but his judgment; and he betrays you instead of serving you, if he sacrifices it to your opinion. You choose a member indeed, but when you have chosen him, he is not a member of Bristol, but he is a member of Parliament."

The difficulties today of living up to this true conception of representative government are manifest. Under our system of direct primaries and direct legislation, the power of organized minorities, with their artificial propaganda, and paid agitators, tends to force members of legislative bodies to represent special elements rather than the great body of their constituency. As President Coolidge said when he was Governor of Massachusetts, "We have had too much legislating by clamor, by tumult, by pressure. Representative government ceases when outside influence of any kind is substituted for the judgment of the representative." It is therefore more important than ever to abide by the representative principle.

The initiative, referendum, and recall are expedients expressing distrust in representative government. The initiative is a method by which a very small portion of the electorate can propose legislation which the legislature has refused to countenance. The measure is presented on petition of a limited number, say five per cent of the voters. It is instigated by a group who generally have some special interest to further. It is an easy matter to get signatures. Many people will sign any petition. The legislation so initiated cannot be changed, even in phraseology; it cannot be amended or perfected; it cannot be examined or discussed before final action is taken. It goes on the ballot as originally drafted, and it must be adopted *in toto* or rejected. Experience has shown that the people take scant interest in these proposals. Only about one-half of those who actually vote for candidates take the trouble to vote on questions submitted to them. If such a measure is adopted, it is by a very small fraction of the electorate — minority rule in its very essence. It is legislation in defiance of the wishes of those chosen to legislate; it is legislation by default.

The compulsory referendum is no more satisfactory. This is the automatic submission to popular vote of acts of the legislature. I do not refer to the limited use of the referendum upon constitutional and other questions of major importance which the people are entitled to pass upon. It is appropriate to ascertain public sentiment on such questions, but to transfer from the legislature to the people the ordinary powers of legislation is wrong in principle and harmful in practice. It destroys the responsibility of the legislature; reduces it to a mere recording agency, a subordinate and subservient body. No self-respecting citizen would care to serve in a body of this character.

It is the function of a legislature to determine the best method of accomplishing a desired result.

A bill, introduced with the best of intentions, may, if enacted into law, do more harm than good. All measures must be examined carefully in committee; evidence thereon must be heard and weighed; bills are often redrafted and amended; and frequently it is seen that they will not accomplish the end sought, and they are rejected. Experience is necessary to prevent ill-considered laws. Wisdom in legislation has to be acquired. The only safeguard against a flood of unnecessary and injurious statutes is full discussion and careful deliberation before a law is enacted. This is assured only through strict adherence to the representative principle.

The recall of public officials, including the judiciary, is a device calculated both to deter high-minded and self-respecting men from accepting election to public office, and to develop a class of unprincipled office seekers who will not hesitate to change their views as the wind blows. As applied to the judiciary, it is particularly pernicious. If there is one safeguard of the rights of the people, it is the independent judiciary. "The judicial department," said Chief Justice Marshall, "comes home in its effects to every man's fireside. It passes on his property, his reputation, his all. Is it not to the last degree important that a judge should be rendered perfectly and completely independent, with nothing to influence or control him but God and his conscience?" Once the judges are made subservient to the popular will, their true function is destroyed, and all our great constitutional rights are in danger. Upon the independence of the judiciary depends the administration of impartial justice, and the decision of causes in accordance with the principles of right, to rich and poor alike, free from prejudice, free from self-interest, without fear of punishment or hope of reward. It is our security of liberty under law.

These attempts to depart from representative government have produced no apparent beneficial results. "After a decade or more of trial and test by actual experience," said Chief Justice Taft, "this adoption of so-called 'purer' democracy has not been a success." The people as a whole have neither the aptitude nor the inclination to govern themselves directly.

The direct primary, which was regarded, when instituted, as a signal advance toward better government, has been a great disappointment. As it has necessitated large expenditures of money, candidates without strong financial backing are severely handicapped. It has weakened party government, and has failed to produce better candidates. Anyone seeking office can enter the primaries and run for a place on the party ticket. He may have no party ties, and if he is nominated and elected, he owes nothing to the party, yet he bears the party label. He is under no obligation to support the party policies. He is masquerading as a member of a party, but he owes it no allegiance.

Without party organization, there can be little effective governmental action. The only way that the divergent political views of different sections, classes, and interests can be reconciled, and consolidated into a concrete form, is through parties. Otherwise, individual groups representing their own special interests would be in continual conflict, and little of benefit to the people as a whole could be accomplished. Party government involves the willingness of these groups to subordinate their particular interests to the good of the greater number.

Munro has said: "The strength of parties is an index of popular interest in public affairs; their weakness and disintegration is a sign of a political indifference among the people."[1] If this is true, any expedient tending to undermine party government should be discountenanced. Parties should be held responsible for their candidates, and candidates should be loyal to their party.

"The most satisfactory working of representative government is secured under a two-party system, one party unitedly supporting the administration, the other presenting a vigorous opposition."[2] In France, where there are numerous parties, there are no clear-cut opposing issues. There are changing coalitions, varying combinations, and no continuity of policy. The result is lack of achievement.

The line of cleavage between the two predominant parties in the United States today is not as clearly defined as it has been in the past. There are no opposing theories of government such as separated the Federalists and Democratic-Republicans of the time of Hamilton and Jefferson, no such absorbing political questions as those of the time of Clay, Webster, and Jackson, no major controversy such as that over the League

[1] W. B. Munro, *The Government of the United States* (N. Y. 1925), p. 367.

[2] *Ibid.*, p. 373.

of Nations. The two parties today encroach upon each other's preserves. There are conservative and radical elements in each. In each there are those who are primarily interested in industry, in labor, in agriculture. Neither on foreign policy, nor on domestic issues, is there any well-defined alignment.

The country is so large, and made up of so many divergent interests with different problems and different points of view that it is very difficult for any one party to satisfy all its constituent parts. In the effort to do so, party platforms have been reduced to mere "glittering generalities," and controversial or embarrassing questions are, for the most part, evaded. Real issues are, if possible, avoided. Both parties are fearful of offending some particular sections, or class, or some powerful organization. There are groups in each party who have little else in common except the use of the party label. Thus, party platforms have become largely mere gestures for the purpose of appeasing all elements in the party, have become to a great extent meaningless, and political parties can no longer be relied upon for effective leadership.

Our hope, therefore, lies in making party government stronger and more responsible, and this can be accomplished best by adhering to the representative principle. Our task is to stimulate a greater interest on the part of the people in public questions. The discussion of political issues through energetic party organizations is an important factor to this end. Political parties, instead of being "mere machines without life or initiative, intent solely on getting into office,"[1] could be made to take the leadership in directing public opinion and crystallizing public sentiment.

If the people are not capable of sustaining a genuinely representative government, then our government is a failure. The alternative of representative government is class government. No system of popular government can be successful unless the people themselves realize fully their obligations of citizenship. This is our goal in America — to impress upon the average individual that the better he fulfills his duties as an American citizen, the better will his government function, and the greater will be his own security, his own prosperity, and his own happiness. The purposes for which the framers met over one hundred and thirty-nine years ago are today our

[1] A. Siegfried, *America Comes of Age*, p. 246.

purposes, and the fundamental principles of government which they adopted are today our fundamental principles. "We, the people of the United States," they said in the Preamble to the Constitution, "in order to form a more perfect union, establish justice, insure domestic tranquillity, provide for the common defence, promote the general welfare, and secure the blessings of liberty to ourselves and our posterity, do ordain and establish this Constitution for the United States of America." The Constitution thus "ordained and established" is today our Constitution; to protect and preserve it from assault is our proud privilege.

INDEX

INDEX